Page 102, line 21, read ⸍ ... ⸍ ... for D.H. Lawrence

Page 119, line 13, read Arthur Schnitzler for Arthur Koestler

Page 127, line 7, read 1,600 for 16,000

ANTI-SEMITISM

PROVOCATIONS

ANTI-SEMITISM

FREDERIC RAPHAEL

SERIES EDITOR:
YASMIN ALIBHAI-BROWN

Biteback Publishing

First published in Great Britain in 2015 by
Biteback Publishing Ltd
Westminster Tower
3 Albert Embankment
London SE1 7SP
Copyright © Frederic Raphael 2015

ISBN 978-1-84954-890-8

10 9 8 7 6 5 4 3 2 1

A CIP catalogue record for this book is available from the British Library.

Set in Stempel Garamond

Printed and bound in Great Britain by
CPI Group (UK) Ltd, Croydon CR0 4YY

Acknowledgements

THIS ESSAY HAS profited immeasurably from the help of my friends, especially Michael Burleigh, whose prompt, precise and sometimes rectifying expertise has been invaluable. George Walden has been typically and unsparingly generous. Joseph Epstein made several knowledgeable suggestions and proposed some neat trims, all of which I have accepted. Dr Gershon Hepner provided me with several telling details. I have been greatly encouraged by Mark Glanville's comments and by the enthusiasm with which James Stephens of Biteback Publishing responded to early drafts. Melissa Bond, of Biteback, has subjected my text to meticulous editorial scrutiny.

My old friend David Pryce-Jones alerted me to several ineptitudes. David introduced me to the literature of European anti-Semitism when, fifty-five years ago, as literary editor of *Time and Tide*, he sent me Raul Hilberg's *The Destruction of the European Jews* for review. It is with affection and an abiding sense of never quite finishing that review that I dedicate this book to a man and writer of rare courage and integrity.

✣ ✣ ✣

I

'How odd / Of God / To choose / The Jews!' William Norman Ewer's pre-Holocaust squib encapsulates one of the oldest of old, old stories. The implication is that a God worth believing in would have known better. The question remains why generation after generation, of never more than a few million human beings, of differing ambitions, appearances, allegiances and locations, have been labelled 'bloody Jews' and lumped together as 'The Enemy' in so many programmes for salvation – religious and social – in this world and the next.

The primary, by no means obsolete, answer is that, in Christian scripture and mythology (if they can be distinguished), the so-called 'Chosen Race' were responsible for the death of the Son of God and deemed to be ejected forever from divine favour. As a result, not the Messiah, but damnation was coming for them. Hitler led Europe on what might be described as 'the Last Crusade'. Now, with the arrogance of Israel and 'the Zionists', it is the pious hope of Muslim fanatics, most television networks (especially the BBC), *The Guardian* and other agencies of virtue that the world's greatest and incorrigible troublemakers will soon be taught a conclusive lesson. Israel has become the Judas state.

Even if, as Richard Dawkins and other pundits and lay-preachers have announced, God does not exist and the Second Coming of Jesus Christ has been adjourned *sine die*, 'the Chosen' retain their base reputation. Dawkins's professorial status lends credibility to his assertion that 'the Jews' control the world's economy and, in particular, the press.[1] This article of faith brooks

---

1 Germany's leading newspaper *Die Welt* reported recently that 'students' were saying that there had to be a million Jews in Frankfurt (actual population just over 700,000). The reason for their conclusion? There were so many banks in the city. It is, of course, possible that this is a German joke.

no empirical refutation. If the overwhelming mass of newspapers and broadcasters continue to abuse Israel (and the academy to ostracise its professors and make life lonely for its supporters), that proves only how clever certain people can be in dissimulating their powers. Like the god in whom Dawkins refuses to believe, the Jews are presumed to move in a mysterious way. The new anti-Semite's version of atheism contrives not to have a cake and to eat it too.

* * *

2

WHERE DID IT start, the damnation of the Jews? 'His blood be on our heads and on the heads of our children!' the Jerusalem mob are reported, by Christian sources, to have cried, with a single voice, when the Roman governor Pontius Pilate hesitated to authorise the crucifixion of Jesus of Nazareth. In truth, what is less likely than Jewish unanimity on any topic? Although the Greeks come a close second, Jews are among the most fractious of human beings. Despite small numbers and cruel experiences, they have preserved their literary culture, cryptic calligraphy and endogamous tendencies since ancient times. They have also shown an inexhaustible capacity for denouncing each other's readings of religious and political rectitude. That *all* Jews should be damned, in so many ancient and modern programmes for human elevation, is evidence, above all, of the interaction of religious and philosophical wishful thinking.

The quarrels of clever Jews have furnished their enemies with easy ammunition. During centuries of Christian oppression, Jewish self-mockery and mutual scorn were barbed with an aggressivity very few dared to express outside the ghetto. 'Jewish self-hatred' serves to endorse anti-Semitism; if they think so little of each other, why should anyone else think better? Karl Marx, the atheist grandson of an eminent rabbi, denounced Ferdinand Lassalle, an articulate critic of Marx's version of salvationary socialism, as an opportunist Yid.

Later, Marx widened his sights to denounce Jews in general as a 'huckster race', pedlars of the parasitic bacillus of capitalism. His manifesto had it that the working class would be the new Chosen People, and the Communist

Party its atheist, non-denominational High Priesthood. Once in power, Lenin made the bourgeoisie his sacrificial beasts. Bertrand Russell would never forget how Vladimir Ilyich insisted on the irrelevance of 'innocence' of those of whom the party chose to make an example. Terror was an early recruit as the midwife of the earthly paradise.

After his outstanding contribution, intellectual and strategic, to the success of the 1917 Bolshevik Revolution, the sophisticated Leon Trotsky (*nom de guerre* of Lev Davidovich Bronshtein), was mortified to discover that the Russian working class, natural vessels of the new morality, shared the 'bourgeois' hatred of Jews, a sentiment sanctified by the Orthodox Church. Under the tsars, Russia's Jews, apart from a very few with rare, desirable qualities, were allowed to live only in the bleak villages of the 'Pale of Settlement'.

When Trotsky challenged Joseph Stalin's rise in the party, he was evicted from his central, heroic (and undeniably mass-murderous) role in the revolution.[2] Comrades Lev Kamenev and Grigory Zinoviev un-Jewed themselves

2 See Stephen Kotkin's *Stalin*, Vol. 1 (2014).

by siding with Stalin.[3] As a Georgian, the ex-seminarian Stalin certified his Russian authenticity and new faith not least by his anti-Semitism. By the end of the 1920s, the exiled Trotsky had become another wandering Jew – militant atheism's Judas. His seditious influence could be blamed whenever and wherever any of Stalin's plans went wrong. Even after Trotsky had been murdered, his sinister influence was said to live on. When Stalinism itself lost intellectual traction, Trotsky's allegedly finer vision of Marxism gained new adherents and survived the collapse of the USSR.

In the 1920s and 1930s, many Jews, inside Russia and elsewhere, continued to vest apocalyptic hopes in Bolshevism. One of Stalin's most pitiless enforcers was Solomon Mikhoels. At the same time, international finance was said to be manipulated, with typical selfishness, by 'the Jews'. Both left and right in post-Great War Europe had loud reason to make Jews their scapegoats of choice. When war was imminent in 1939, 'Bendor', the Duke of Westminster, England's richest landlord, held 'the Jews'

---

3 They were later star defendants in the rigged 'show trials' of the 1930s, in which they were convicted and sentenced to death for plotting against Stalin. They were executed in August 1936. Kamenev was Trotsky's brother-in-law.

responsible. The Cliveden Set and the glamour of Sir Oswald ('Tom') and Lady Mosley lent more aristocratic support to His Grace's diagnosis. As the Jews of Europe were hounded and abused, the Walrus and the Carpenter did not lack equivalents either in *Debrett's* and *Who's Who* or among readers of the *Daily Mail*. After Hitler announced that the Jews had it coming to them, he was not short of sympathisers in London.

The rise and abrupt fall of Leslie Hore-Belisha, one of the most energetic and clever of Neville Chamberlain's ministers at the outbreak of war, supply the cruel comedy needed to exemplify how deep and unwarranted was the scorn felt for any Jew (albeit heroic in the Great War). 'Chips' Channon, the Chicago-born epitome of the social-climbing *arriviste* of the 1930s, aped his betters' view of Hore-Belisha by terming him an 'oily Jew'. However, when the Glasgow socialist Emanuel Shinwell was told, in the House of Commons, to 'go back to Poland where you came from', he crossed the floor and slapped the Tory Commander Robert Tatton Bower across the face. Sporting enough to play the blind eyewitness, the Speaker claimed not to have seen the incident.

❊   ❊   ❊

3

THE JEWS HAVE long had difficulties in going back where at least some of them came from. Their divisions and dispersal began in 722 BCE, when – according to the second Book of Kings, chapters 17 and 18 – the Assyrians defeated the Northern Kingdom and ten of the original twelve tribes lapsed from the historical record.[4] The solidarity of the surviving two tribes was riven with deportations, rivalries and civil wars. At least some of the Jews who sat down and wept in Babylon later made the best of a bad job. Baghdad remained a centre of Jewish activity and scholarship until well into the twentieth century.

In the first century BCE, the Romans became the colonial authority in charge of Jerusalem only as the result of a dispute between two brothers, descendants of the

---

4   They continued to have various forms of mythological existence. In the eighteenth century, the Japanese, the American Indians, some African tribes and even the British were identified with the lost tribes (London was taken to be a version of Le Dan, 'belonging to the tribe of Dan'). According to solemn theories, some proposed by Christian sects, the Messiah would not come until he could celebrate the reconciliation of Israel. The Jews had, as it were, to pull themselves together if the return of Jesus was not to remain an unredeemed promise. Meanwhile, they were spoiling everybody's party. This maquette has now been adjusted to serve modern geopolitics.

freedom-fighting Maccabees. A century earlier, the legendary brothers had detached Judaea from the Hellenistic Seleucid monarchy. Pompey the Great was invited to come and settle a competition for the throne between Aristobulus (last king of the Maccabean dynasty) and his ineffectual brother Hyrcanus, the High Priest. A third party, of fundamentalist Jews, hoped that Pompey would rid them of the apparatus of mundane monarchy and install a theocracy[5] in which, as in the Ayatollahs' Iran, the priesthood would provide the masters of life and death.

Pompey and his legions broke away from the lucrative conquest of Syria and, in the hope of quick gold, attacked Jerusalem on the Sabbath, doubtless after being tipped off that Jews were forbidden by God's laws to raise a hand on the Seventh Day, even in self-defence.[6] This rule, with its potentially suicidal consequence, had been suspended by one of the original Maccabeans during their war against the Hellenistic monarchy of the Seleucids; but the ortho-

---

5 An ultra-orthodox segment of today's Israeli society refuses to acknowledge the authority of the secular Jewish state and claims exemption from military service. Like France's Muslims, its followers have unusually large families and pose what some regard as a demographic threat.

6 Pompey was amazed and somewhat awed to find that, in the Holy of Holies in the blood-stained Temple of Jerusalem, there was literally nothing. The solitary Jewish God had no statue and no sumptuous décor.

dox continued to allow no excuse for any activity, even the lighting of a match, on the Seventh Day.[7]

Down the years, enemies of the Jews have not failed to take advantage of this sacred embargo. In 1973, the President of Egypt attacked Israel on Yom Kippur, the holiest day of the Jewish religious calendar. For this stratagem, Anwar Sadat was applauded by the Arab world and cheered on by Arnold Toynbee, the English historical pundit, who declared himself blessed with second sight (he claimed to have had eyewitness access to the Battle of Marathon in 490 BCE). Sadat's early victory was followed by condign defeat, which, thanks to Golda Meir's diplomacy, he was able to pass off as a success. Sadat's show of martial kudos allowed him to make peace with the Israelis. He was received hospitably in Jerusalem and, more important for hungry Egyptians, blessed

---

7 After stumbling across Rava-Ruska, location of a Second World War prison camp for French soldiers in Ukraine, where his paternal grandfather was interned, Father Patrick Desbois, a Roman Catholic priest from France, devoted his life to revealing in Ukraine, Belarus, Moldova, Romania and Poland the mass graves where more than a million Jews were buried, many of them alive. He addressed a group of Jews in Beverly Hills on 19 April 1925, and told the following story. A Ukrainian, whom he was interviewing during the course of his search for mass graves of Jews murdered by *Einsatzgruppen* during the *Shoah*, asked him whether he thought he would go to hell for his sins. 'Which sins do you refer to?' asked Father Desbois. 'The sin of working on Sunday,' replied the Ukrainian. 'I used to make doors for the gas chambers in Belzec,' he explained, 'and was compelled to perform this work not only during the week, but on Sundays.' Gershon Hepner alerted me to this anecdote.

with large American subventions. His pragmatism rendered Sadat a pariah among brother Arabs, for whom coming to terms with the Jews mounted to apostasy. In 1981, while on the podium during a parade to celebrate his 1973 triumph, he was shot by one of his own bodyguards. In 1951, King Abdullah I of Jordan, who favoured a live-and-let's-prosper accommodation with Israel, had been assassinated at Friday prayers in Jerusalem, by a Palestinian gunman.

* * *

4

THE NEW TESTAMENT gives the impression that the Son of God was crowned with thorns and put to death only because of cruel pressure put on the humane Pilate by 'the Jews'. Christian theologians, such as Richard Bauckham in his award-winning *Jesus and the Eyewitnesses* (2006), maintain that the Gospels derive from contemporary, dispassionate evidence. In practice, any lawyer knows that eyewitnesses often testify to what confirms their own preconceptions or advances their case. The eye is a selective organ; 'beliefs' supply rosy or distorting lenses. When it comes to religion or ideology (its secular double), evidence is regularly tailored to fit premeditated conclusions. Baruch (Benedict) Spinoza (1632–77) became disillusioned with Judaism not least because, as a precocious Hebrew scholar, he could prove that the Torah was not written by a single, inspired author. His doubts about anyone receiving divine dictation were limited, for prudent reasons, to Moses and the Torah, but they apply, *mutatis mutandis*, with equal force to the claims of the New Testament to embody the unmitigated word of God. 'Gospel truth' is an unacknowledged oxymoron.

The crucifixion of Jesus or any other 'native' troublemaker could not possibly have been ordered or carried out by 'the Jews'. Roman governors were given to the summary despatch of local troublemakers; but they and they alone made those decisions. Little more than a decade after the death of Jesus, a pseudo-prophet called Theudas acquired a credulous Jewish following, which he led to the River Jordan where he promised a Moses-style parting of the waters. One of Pilate's successors had Theudas decapitated. This led to the deflation of his enthusiasts.

The futility of trying to kill an immortal was proved, so Christians believe, by the discovery that, three days after His crucifixion, Jesus had risen from the tomb and ascended bodily into heaven. Saintly and polemic Christian Fathers soon contrived to exempt Roman officials from complicity in his death.[8] The transfer of blood-guilt left 'the Jews' solely and conveniently responsible. At the same time, it could not be denied, except by frantic cranks, that Jesus was a Jew whose teachings derived almost entirely from what became the Old Testament.[9] According to an annex to Catholic dogma, confirmed in 1950 by Pope Pius XII, His ascent into heaven was followed by the 'Assumption' of the Blessed Virgin Mary to the same destination. This unarguable (because *ex cathedra*) decision was backed by reference not only to St Paul's letter to the Corinthi-

---

8 The soldiers who hammered in the nails and played dice for Jesus's robe were only doing their job and behaving as squaddies always will.

9 In the 1940s, Ludwig Wittgenstein – who had been baptised a Catholic but was, so to say, re-Judaised by Nazi definition – 'confessed' that his seemingly innovative and irreligious philosophical style was '100 per cent Hebraic'. His quondam Viennese neighbour Sigmund Freud made it clear that 'whereof one cannot speak' can remain a muscular, if 'sub-conscious', element in the language. Carlo Michelstaedter anticipated his peers in identifying this as the '*logos alogos*', the unspoken aspect of a given logic.

ans, but also to a passage in Genesis, chapter 3, verse 15. Hebrew scriptures hold an ineradicable place in Christian claims to divine election.

During the Third Reich, the same Pope Pius had decided against public condemnation of Nazi anti-Semitism. To excommunicate Hitler or any of his henchmen might 'confuse' the German faithful. In the 1930s, the Nazi regime had mimicked antique Catholic practice by burning books by Jewish authors. Between 1941 and 1945, the Germans and their helpers exceeded the zeal even of the Holy Inquisition in burning people. Some six million Jews (a quarter of them children) were shot or gassed. When time pressed, or for fun, babies were thrown alive into the furnaces of the crematoria. The pleasures of persecution rarely excite comment. Fanatics are always taken to be, if nothing else, *sincere*. In fact, from top to bottom, the whole Holocaust enterprise yielded literally golden opportunities for theft, as well as for rape, promotion and the avoidance of front-line service. No one who works in an abattoir needs to hate sheep.

In due time, academic 'authorities' (Noam Chomsky among them) declared that the existence of the gas chambers was questionable. Chomsky later claimed that he had endorsed the *right* to question whether the Holocaust had taken place, but that he had not seconded, for instance, the Franco-British academic Robert Faurisson's claim (in 1979) that it was a fabrication. The zeal of some of the latter's supporters continues to suggest, as do other 'respectable', sometimes Jewish academics, a 'sub-conscious' wish that the Jews themselves were responsible for what happened to them or, even better, for what didn't.

*   *   *

5

IN THE FIRST century CE, Jews made up around 10 per cent of the population of the Roman world. Judaism might be regarded as an outlandish religion (Emperor Caligula, in jocular mood, asked a Jewish delegation what aberration led them to forgo the pleasure of roast pork), but in Rome and other major cities around the Mediterranean, synagogues attracted many 'tourists', including Poppaea Sabina, wife of Emperor Nero. There were fewer proselytes, not least because Judaism has never been hot to recruit other people or, as Christianity and Islam have, to impose itself by force.[10]

The largest concentration of Jews outside Jerusalem was in Alexandria. That city's mostly Hellenised Hebrews took no part in the uprising in Judaea, which reached its climax in 70 CE, when Vespasian and his son Titus sacked Jerusalem.[11] The ensuing executions were limited to 7,000, only by a shortage of wood for crosses. The High Priest and his acolytes were evicted from the Temple of Herod the Great. Jews were deprived of a central place of worship and of an official hierarchy; captives were herded into camps. Rabbis became mendicant teachers, dependent on bookish erudition, not on robed splendour, to keep the Word alive. Prayer, which had been communal, became a form of worship that could take place anywhere and in

---

10 The only obvious case of enforced conversion was that of the Idumaeans – 'tribesmen' who lived in the region of the modern Negev desert. They were conscripted in the second century BCE by the Maccabees to augment their numbers in fighting the Seleucid king Antiochus IV and his successors. The Idumaeans came to play a determinant, unhappy role in the siege of Jerusalem in 69 CE. The conversion of the Turkic Kazars in the Middle Ages (the subject of Arthur Koestler's wishful essay 'The Thirteenth Tribe') was due to the decision of their ruler that Judaism was true and its distortionate derivatives, Christianity and Islam, were not. For a dramatised account, see Yehuda Halevi's *The Kuzari*, written in Judaeo-Arabic in twelfth century Al-Andalus.

11 His chief of staff, Tiberius Julius Alexander, was an apostate Jew from Alexandria who had no conscientious reluctance to out-Roman the Romans in putting down the rebellion.

solitude.[12] Vespasian forbade the construction of a temple at Leontopolis in Egypt, but he refused to take any measures against, for instance, Alexandrian Jews in general, although their enemies were quick to solicit their abasement. Like many people or peoples, Jews may have been disliked in the ancient world,[13] but there was no widespread, articulate philosophy of malice against them before the rise of institutional Christianity.

In 135 CE, Bar-Kochba's rebellion attempted yet again to detach Judaea from the Roman Empire. The victorious Emperor Hadrian was more vindictive even than his triumphant predecessors. Jerusalem was renamed Aelia Capitolina and dedicated to Zeus;[14] Jews were denied entrance to it. Their humiliation was soon retailed in Christian publicity as proof that the once Chosen People had forfeited divine favour. In time, this de-selection would be fashioned into they-asked-for-it justification for anathemas, ghettoisation, *pogroms* and, eventually,

---

12 I am grateful to Michael Burleigh for this point, as for many others.

13 See, for instances, Peter Schäfer, *Judaeophobia* (1997).

14 Hadrian was so keen a Hellenist that he seldom went to Rome. After the Arab conquest of Palestine, the Al-Aqsa Mosque was built where Herod's Temple had stood. To emphasise its sacred character, the Prophet was said to have ascended into heaven, as had Elijah in Jewish scripture, from the roof of the mosque. Impartial sources question whether, in truth, Muhammad ever went to Jerusalem at all.

genocide. God the Father was deemed to have passed sentence on His previously Chosen People. They had failed to recognise, and then 'betrayed', His son. Their subsequent sufferings proved that the God was in His heaven. Matching Caesar, He had given the Jews the thumbs-down in the world's arena.

Three centuries after the crucifixion of Jesus, Constantine the Great converted himself and impelled his subjects to a version of Christianity. Endorsement of monotheism did not inhibit the *arriviste* emperor from the construction of a temple to advertise the divinity of his own family. His purposes were less evangelistic than homogenising. It suited the upstart to claim the sponsorship of an omnipotent deity (eyewitnesses claimed to have seen a cross in the sky at the decisive Battle of the Milvian Bridge) and to enrol the citizens of a disparate empire in what was to become a more-or-less common ritual. The hope was that an empire that prayed together would stay together. Religious practice and social cohesion are closely related.[15] It would be wrong to suppose that Constantine intended all

---

15 The Englishness of Anglicanism announced in whose premises, so to say, the power and the glory were vested. It was a good career move for 'natives' to become Christian. George Orwell, when a colonial policeman, was amazed when an Indian declared, without apparent shame, 'I am a *Joo*, sir!' How many Etonians would have done as much?

the consequences of his executive, somewhat impromptu decision; but he set in motion a trend that led to Rome becoming the centre of the Catholic Church. The papacy then assumed what Chinese sages called 'the mandate of heaven'. The city that had conquered the pagan Mediterranean by force took over the spiritual hegemony of Christendom. Bishops and cardinals became the legates and proconsuls of the Supreme Pontiff, who inherited his title from the (elected) chief priests of pagan Rome – Julius Caesar among them.

The argument between Judaism and its mutation, Christianity, assumed the ruthlessness of a civil war. Each side understood the other only too well. Violent internal antagonisms were a loud part of the history of the early Church.[16] For several centuries, there was no precise definition of what Christians believed, or had to believe, apart from according messianic status to Jesus Christ (and looking forward to His imminent return to earth). The followers of Arius, an influential third- and fourth-century Alexandrian Christian thinker, doubted the Son's essential equality with God the Father. After their views were declared heretical at the

---

16 See, for instances, Brent Shaw's *Sacred Violence: African Christians and Sectarian Hatred in the Age of Augustine* (2011).

Council of Nicaea in 325 CE, Arians were often referred to, for instance by St Augustine, as 'Jews'. The epithet 'Jew' became a muddy term that any preacher could stick on any enemy; you never had to be one to be called one.[17] All the money-lenders patronised by Lord Byron (several of them Scots, like himself) were so labelled by the unmalicious poet, whose *Hebrew Melodies*, with modernised music by Isaac Nathan, amounted to a hymnal for proto-Zionists.

After the establishment of the papacy, pagan Rome's hostility was not held against the descendants, Italian or otherwise, of those who had thrown martyrs to the lions, or did them to death in other entertaining ways. Myth favours a single brand of villain. Mimicking the ancient circus, the Christian *auto-da-fé* would turn the roasting of Jews and heretics into occasions for morbid solemnity and the celebration of self-righteousness.[18] If enough injustices are committed in the name of a cause, it becomes unthinkable that it not be true.

---

17 In denouncing the Jacobins after the French Revolution of 1789, Edmund Burke tagged them 'Jews', even though not one was of Semitic origin. Rhetoric is not a science. Anti-Semitism, void of observation of actual Jews, became a part of civilised speech.

18 According to Cecil Roth, author of *The Spanish Inquisition* (1937), the Holy Office chose to incinerate its victims in order to avoid having priests soil their hands with blood. Islamic executioners wear rubber gloves for the same fastidious reason.

Public executions also played an early part in the rise of the third monotheism: Islam. When the Jews, yet again, declined to endorse the Prophet's message, Muhammad personally supervised the beheading of 700 male Jews, whose crime was not to have rallied to Allah. Their women and children were consigned to slavery. Christians and Muslims continued to make a virtue of massacring Jews, who lacked either the appetite or the numbers to reciprocate. Yet neither of the later monotheisms could ever quite deny the fundamental role of the Jews as People of the Book.[19]

It is a recurrent element of the polemic against Israel to declare that it has conducted 'massacres', though none has been confirmed by impartial evidence.[20] The English literary journalist A. N. Wilson (who has asserted that Israel 'poisons water supplies') announced that, by attacking

---

19 The Aztecs became the overwhelming power in Central America after they had driven out the previously dominant tribe, the Toltecs. The Aztecs built themselves a great city (Tenochtitlan was finer than Venice, said one of the conquistadors who observed its pillage), but – despite their programme of mass sacrifice of other defeated tribes to their insatiable deity – they retained an incurable, superstitious regard for the Toltecs, who had been exiled to a remote region. The Aztecs sent frequent messengers to ask the Toltec 'oracle' whether they were well regarded by their gods. The diminished Toltecs never failed to disappoint their opulent, but nervous conquerors.

20 The massacre in Sabra and the Chatilla refugee camp in 1982, where 'between 762 and 3,500' Shi'ites are said to have died, was carried out by the Lebanese Christian Falange. The odium has, however, been attached almost exclusively, and happily, to the Israeli general Ariel Sharon (the principal victor over Sadat in 1973), who did nothing to stop the killing. Pontius Pilate, of whom Christians say something similar, has received a better press.

a notorious base for suicide bombers in Jenin, the Israel Defense Forces (IDF) were guilty of 'massacre … genocide … immense slaughter'. A report from the UN (rarely even-handed when it comes to Israel) conceded, rather late in the day, that no massacre took place at Jenin. There had been a battle between Israelis and well-armed Palestinian fighters, with similar, not very great, numbers of casualties on both sides.

The fact that Christianity and, to a lesser degree, Islam rely on the primordial books of the Jews generated a schizophrenia that at once concedes and seeks to efface the primacy of Judaism. Confident of their monopoly on the means of salvation, the second and third monotheisms have sought, by fire and sword, to impose their machinery on the world. Jews, who have never done so, are accused by both of an appetite for global domination, which neither Islam nor Christianity denies. Unlike evangelical Protestants, who are strong for Israel, another strain of meta-Christians and most Muslim enthusiasts have a need for 'the Zionists' to be guilty of the kind of bloody crimes that have been visited on Jews, without reprisal, down the centuries. The historian Lewis Namier, who chose to specialise in the political minutiae of Georgian society, was once asked why he never wrote about 'his own people'. His reply was that Jews didn't have a history, 'only a martyrology'.

Muslims were, from the inception of their faith, contributors to the long river of Jewish blood.[21] In 1066, 3,000–6,000 Jews were slaughtered in Granada, where the Moorish emir had made one of them, Samuel ibn Naghrela, his vizier. Naghrela, who had renovated the Alhambra, was crucified by a Muslim mob. Anti-Semitic mythology requires the view that Naghrela and his co-religionists must have done something very wrong to deserve being put to the sword. Innocence is never attributed to what A. N. Wilson calls 'hate-filled' Jews by Christians, Muslims and their discriminating adherents.

Manifestly docked of divine favour by their eviction from Jerusalem, 'the Jews' became prime suspects whenever misfortune struck God's new, and only, favourites – the Christians. Jews were sealed by pious logic into an identity from which there could be no escape, except by conversion.[22] Their refusal to bow down to the image

---

21 For further instances, see *In Ishmael's House* (2011) by Martin Gilbert.

22 With the advent of 'racial' vanities, beginning with the fifteenth-century Hispanic fantasy of 'pure blood' and culminating in the twentieth-century myth of Aryan supremacy, Jews lost even the prospect of shedding their alien miasma by baptism.

of Jesus Christ made them the terrestrial, if landless, representatives of the Devil. In the eyes of venerable figures, from St Augustine to Blaise Pascal, Jews were suffered to survive, in dark corners of the earth, only to provide proof, by their heaven-sent degradation, that Christianity was the one true faith. The magnificence of Christian churches flaunted the evidence of divine favour. The gilded sumptuousness of the papacy became an aspect of His grace.

Christian theologians did, however, have problems when mundane misfortune descended on the faithful. If God served the Jews right by delivering Jerusalem to the Romans, why did He allow 'innocent' people to suffer? To posit a perpetual Jewish conspiracy saved the 'logical' sum of things. In our time, the Jewish 'lobby' is, by the same token, regularly accused of being the sole agency responsible for the misfortunes of, in particular, the people of the Middle East, and also for the price of motoring.

The only plausible reason for the ineptitudes of post-war western governments, as far back at 1956, has to be that their minds have been poisoned by Jewish influences.

❊   ❊   ❊

6

S T JOHN'S *'LOGOS'* is translated, in the King James
Bible, neatly but incompletely, as 'the Word'. In Greek,
logos can also imply the source of a logical system. The
divine *logos* that validated Christianity had a second life
in European philosophy, into which both St Augustine
and Pascal were enrolled, as it were, as honorary colonels.
Religious dogma mutated into the notion of logic as an
impersonal regulator of human thought, against which,
as in mathematics, there could be no appeal. While the
philosopher took on the allure, if rarely the practice, of a
dispassionate and implacable analyst, European philosophy never ceased to pulse with undeclared preconceptions.

In the Enlightenment, 'the Jews' were transposed into
a scandalous[23] element in the grammar of civilisation. A
line of philosophers, mainly German, from the benevo-
lent Immanuel Kant, via Hegel and Heidegger, to the Nazi

---

23 The Greek *'skandalon'* means first a 'trap' and hence a 'stumbling block' – an impedi-
ment to smooth progress. John Murray Cuddihy's seemingly amiable *The Ordeal of
Civility* (1975) depicts Jews as outsiders who lack the manners and morals of civilised
people and must qualify for admission.

legal apologist Carl Schmitt, argued the Jews into a men-
ace to the health of the German/Aryan 'race' (a category
without the smallest scientific validity). Schmitt admitted
that the 'religion' of ethnicity required that the Jews fur-
nish a polar 'other' against which Germans might be united
in a fight for survival. The resulting murderous ruthlessness served as a 'necessary' unifying element.[24] The guilt,
or even the genius, of actual individual Jews was not relevant to the essential argument. In logic, consistency passes
for justice. On one of his rare visits to the killing fields of
Nazism, Heinrich Himmler was distressed to see a blonde
girl of remarkable beauty, standing naked on the edge of a
mass grave into which she would fall, a few minutes later,
after being shot. He was sure she must have had Aryan
blood in her veins. When she denied it, he was sorry; but
there was nothing he could do.

No humbug has been more eagerly circulated than the
notion that the Nazi programme, first of eviction, then of
annihilation of the Jews, owed more to the Enlightenment

---

24 Until Prussia's 1870 victory over France, Germany was divided into small principali-
ties. Bismarck then coerced the German states into a single empire. Previously, in the
Thirty Years' War (1618–48), German Catholics and Protestants fought a war of conspicuous internecine savagery. No 'single' nation was in greater need than Germany of
the vainglorious adhesive of military and 'racial' superiority.

than to Christianity. The formal notion of 'anti-Semitism', as a politico-social programme, may date only from 1879, when it was articulated by the German radical Wilhelm Marr, but there is clear continuity between the Christian abhorrence of Jews and the political movement, backed by a Christian population of both Lutherans and Roman Catholics, for Jewish elimination. Strict etymology defines the latter term as territorial eviction, but it elided easily into physical extinction. The political anti-Semitism of the nineteenth century furnished common ground on which German Christians of radically opposed creeds were able to unite.

Bismarck's *Kulturkampf* was aimed deliberately, and loudly, at reducing the influence and dignity of Germany's large Roman Catholic minority. Germany's vanity was better served by Martin Luther's quasi-indigenous Christianity, as Britain's was by the Anglicanism headed by its monarch. Marr's polemic set out to replace Germany's religious segmentation with common ethnicity. The charm and the violence of his polemics were equally seductive. There is small comedy in noting that three of his wives were of Jewish origin.

'Anti-Zionism' is the latest mutation of the malice that

furnishes opportunities for ideological ruthlessness. The 'new' anti-Semitism emits a very old smell. The sins of the Jews have become Israeli crimes and are no less damnable.[25] Post-Christian philosophies proposed various systems of salvation – social and political. They were often alike only in their need for a recognisable threat, in order to create regimental solidarity among 'the saved'. Semantic economy contrived that the old devil and the new both emerge from the same dark corner. First religiously, then politically, 'the Jews' were depicted as the poisonous thorn in the world's flesh. The Roman Catholic missal had always damned the Jews as 'perfidious'; *Mein Kampf* followed suit. The religious stigma was deleted only in 1963 by the not loudly applauded decision of Pope John XXIII's Second Vatican Council (the latter-day recusant Evelyn Waugh deplored all 'modernisation' that deprived him of the comfort of election). For almost two millennia, to brand Jews as the incorporation of 'the enemies of God' was a formula as adaptable as it proved lethal.

The recurrent malice of Christian myth puts its signature

---

25 There is no intention here to claim any monopoly of merit for Jews in general or to deny that Jews and Israelis can behave badly, contemptibly, cruelly or foolishly. They are, after all, human.

on what Norman Cohn called the 'warrant for genocide'. His 1966 study of the same name centred on the fraudulent document known as *The Protocols of the Elders of Zion*. Compiled in Russia at the beginning of the twentieth century, this paranoid fabrication became the New Testament of murderous and self-righteous anti-Semitism. It purported to contain the minutes of the meetings of the leaders of 'the Jewish conspiracy' for world conquest through control of the economy and the press. As long ago as 1921, *The Times* of London established that the document was a forgery; but it continues to dress, and seem to bless, malign purposes.[26]

During the 1930s, Henry Ford, a capitalist whose mass-produced motor cars dominated the US market, distributed half a million copies of *The Protocols*. Ford's favourite preacher Father Charles Coughlin used his weekly radio show to attack communism and capitalism and to blame the Jews for both. For anti-Semites, and now anti-Zionists, the veracity of the falsehood has become an article of faith. In *Mein Kampf*, Hitler proclaimed that 'the Big Lie'[27] was eas-

---

26 Tertullian's dictum re: Christianity, '*credo quia impossibile*' (I believe because it's not possible), has been modernised into '*credo quia falsum*' (I believe it because it's untrue).

27 Both Hitler and Goebbels were admirers of the works of Edward Bernays (1891–1995), the German-born Jewish-American pioneer of the mass-selling techniques that lay behind Hitler's notion of the potency of 'the Big Lie'.

ier for the masses to swallow than any accumulation of small truths. During Hosni Mubarak's tyranny, official Egyptian television (along with other Arab stations) broadcast a thirteen-part dramatisation of *The Protocols*. The wish for the protocols to be genuine serves to promote their counterfeit currency. For twenty years, Barack Obama sat comfortably in a church in Chicago where the resident (black) preacher, Jeremiah Wright, not infrequently denounced the pernicious influence of the Jews in the world.

The part Jews played in the civil rights movement has been as deliberately excised in black history as were the contributions of Jews to European culture by the Nazis. In the 2014 film *Selma,* the laundered version of Martin Luther King is seen marching from Montgomery to Selma accompanied by an unnamed Greek Orthodox priest. Rabbi Abraham Heschel, who walked arm in arm with Martin Luther King all the way, has been deleted from the story, as Trotsky was from Stalinist accounts of the revolution.[28]

---

28 For a paradigm example of emancipated, black American, anti-Jewish attitudes, see Mary Lefkowitz's *History Lesson* (2008). In 1993, a black professor at Wellesley, Tony Martin, had published *The Jewish Onslaught: Despatches from the Wellesley Battlefront*, in which he alleged a conspiracy against him by the usual people. He also wrote a book about what he claimed, with scant evidence, was the large part of Jews in the African slave trade. How much did it say about the very large Arab involvement or about the willingness with which some Africans exploited and exported others?

The protocols have been recycled by European intellectuals, left and right, into an authorised version of contemporary geopolitics that denies the state of Israel the right to exist. Zionism is said by journalists, academics, meta-Marxists and Muslim 'clerics' to represent a unique threat to world peace. To question this view is registered as a symptom of Islamophobia, a leprous social disease akin to 'racism'. According to nice modern cant, the Jews are *not* a race, hence they cannot, in the USA, benefit from the interdiction against public criticism of other supposedly generic groups. For fans of fanaticism, the not uncommon Muslim/Arab desire to wipe Israel – and why not all Jews? – from the face of the earth proves only how gravely Zionism has offended. Israelis (and their friends) are now, by definition, the world's only 'racists'.

❊   ❊   ❊

7

THE 'JUDAEO-CHRISTIAN TRADITION' embodies an antagonism between Church and Synagogue, which shows of inter-faith fraternity or collegial scholarship cannot quite digest. If Christian apologists were to concede that there could be several paths to God, uncomfortable light would play on Catholic (and Calvinist) authoritarianism down the centuries. Jews have not been the only victims of Christian militants. The Mayan and Incan civilisations of South and Central America were put down – their sacred books burned, their works of art melted down – to hasten, as it turned out, the ruinous inflation of Spain. 'Indians' were enslaved or murdered on a warrant signed and sealed by God's Vicar in Rome. Contemporary moral cartographers, who edit the geography of the Middle East in the light of their own conception of distributive justice, are the scribbling successors of the Borgia Pope Alexander VI, who, in May 1493, literally drew the line that allocated South America to the crowns of Portugal and Castile.

When Pope Urban II proclaimed the First Crusade in 1096, German knights rallied to his call. On their way to take ship for the Holy Land, they lent a sharp edge to piety by pillaging and massacring the Jewish communities of the Rhineland, who (unlike the Saracens) lacked the means to defend themselves. On capturing Jerusalem, the crusaders killed local residents without discriminating between their religious affiliations. Successive crusaders slaughtered Muslims with pious application and the promise of paradise.

Today's counter-crusading Islamic State makes matching offers, with carnal embellishments. Trainee martyrs are incited to the sadistic slaughter not only of Christians and other infidels, but also of captive deviants from their own chosen brand of Islam. In the Middle East, recent and continuing struggles between Muslims and other non-Jewish inhabitants of the region have caused something like half a million deaths, many of non-combatants and 'hostages'. The determination by certain Muslims to kill anyone who stands in the way of a second caliphate excites limited outrage among western intellectuals, academics and journalists. If such a programme is regrettable, it must have been excited by Zionists and their agents in the US government.

To suggest that Islam might be anything but the religion of peace (as its name implies) can be taken to be a sign of Islamophobia.[29] For those like Jon Snow and Robert Fisk,

---

29 During the brave days of the Soviet Union, western communists took exception to the idea that *Pravda*, the party newspaper, did not necessarily print 'the truth', as its title insisted. Petronius Arbiter, Nero's aristocratic playmate, observed in the *Satyricon* that Rome had turned the world into a desert and called it peace.

it is a symptom of paranoia to suggest that detestation of Israel has anything in common with anti-Semitism.[30] Yet the millennial they-asked-for-it rubric leers over the scene – a sour vestige of the smile of Lewis Carroll's Cheshire Cat. Israel has become the enemy of choice of latter-day evangelists, who proclaim that the peace of the world is imperilled solely by its existence. Günter Grass, the left-wing German author who died in the spring of 2015, made this accusation with all the moral authority of a Nobel Prize-winner who had also been a member of Hitler's Waffen SS, to whose members the Ulster English poet Tom Paulin likened the Israelis. That Paulin was then accused of prejudice led him to complain of having been 'dealt the anti-Semitic card'.

Reupholstered as Zionists, Jews constitute the sole political 'other' whose extinction would bring harmony to mankind and who, meanwhile, are still badged with the ghost of the Yellow Star. The Christian notion of sal-vation, traditionally delayed only by the obstinacy of the Jews, has metastasised into an ethical doctrine. Islam and the new left share the wish to return the Jews of Israel, if

---

30 Stanley Kubrick defined paranoia as 'knowing what's going on'.

any survive, to the vagrant pariahdom they claim to be their sole due state.

This anti-Zionism is a form of nostalgia for days when Jews were given no choice but to be ashamed of themselves.[31] It requires no refined wit to see, once again, how old myths are recycled: according to today's anti-Zionists, the newest Jerusalem will be purged of Jews and *that* is how world peace will be procured for everyone else. No one was more influential than the late Edward Said in swinging academic and journalistic support behind the Palestinians. Who now cares to mention that, had he survived to live in today's brave new Arab world, he would, as a Christian, have an odds-on chance of being murdered by those whose cause he advocated with such verbose fervour?[32]

---

31 The minor Tory minister, diarist, one-time motor-racing amateur and millionaire cocksman Alan Clark took – and, no doubt, gave – pleasure in contrasting 'British racing green' with 'Jewish racing yellow' – an unsubtle way of qualifying Jews as innate cowards. The refusal of Israelis to turn the other cheek is not the least of their modern sins. Just before her death in 2006, Oriana Fallaci denounced the Italian enemies of Israel, who craved the return of the amenable cosmopolitan Jew.

32 Said's reliance on, especially, Michel Foucault (who endorsed the 'people's justice' of the Iranian Revolution) is characteristic of intellectual assimilationism. Susan Sontag's lifelong ambition was to pass for a French intellectual by displays of paradoxical effrontery. Pol Pot learned his ruthless 'philosophy' in Paris and put it into practice, millions of times, in Cambodia's killing fields.

✳   ✳   ✳

8

THE ACCURSED ROLE of 'the Jews' was sealed into Christian mythology by the accusation that they were responsible for His betrayal.[33] To nail it home, the whole 'race' came to impersonate Judas Iscariot. The Synoptic Evangelists – Jews Matthew and Mark, and the Gentile Luke – are held, by their quasi-convergence, to have established the story of the treachery of Judas Iscariot.[34] St John made Judas the archetypal Jew, willing to do anything for money. As far back as the early third century CE, the Church Father Tertullian, a verbose blogger *avant la lettre*, included, among the pleasures of 'the saved', that of having front-row seats from which to

---

33 Enoch Powell, a Biblical scholar as well as a right-wing politician, conceded that the Jews were never empowered to crucify anyone. Powell then restored the notion of Jewish responsibility by suggesting that Jesus may not have been crucified at all, but rather stoned to death by 'the Jews' (in accordance with their traditional methods of execution). In order to avoid the consequent odium, Jesus was then reported, falsely, to have been crucified by the Romans. The Jewish control of 'the press', it seems, allowed this allegation to become, quite literally, Gospel. See Powell's *The Evolution of the Gospel* (1994).

34 Biblical scholars generally agree that Mark supplied the ur-Gospel on which the others rely.

relish the endless barbecue of unbelievers, and of Judas, in particular.

The fantasy of abstracting Jesus from 'the Jews' is a recurrent obsession with their enemies. The followers of Adolf Hitler, who was portrayed as a crusader in literally shining armour, recycled Jesus into a blond, blue-eyed Aryan. The latter's most recent reincarnation is as a Palestinian (non-Jewish, if still Semitic). It was a long, sacred habit – later a philosophical pleasantry, then a political ploy – to typify 'the Jews' as the fathers of all lies; hence, when they seek to defend themselves, they cannot possibly be telling the truth. The ancient Greeks had a proverb that said the same of Cretans,[35] but more as a folkloric joke (like the one that says, 'Taffy was a Welshman, Taffy was a thief') than as a pronouncement of eternal ostracism. In neo-Nazi and fellow-travelling (both right- and left-wing) propaganda, Holocaust denial becomes an article of faith. All evidence to the contrary is said to derive from Jewish sources.

---

35 Nevertheless, the Cretans, like the Toltecs, had a time-honoured claim to ancient wisdom. In his last work, *The Laws*, Plato replaces his usual interlocutor, Socrates, with a sage described as the Cretan Stranger. The Provençal 'prophet' Nostradamus, whose elastic predictions continue to fascinate the credulous, was of Jewish origin. Gotthold Lessing's character *Nathan the Wise* was an emblematic figure in the (attempted) redemption of the image of 'the Jew' in late eighteenth-century Germany.

In modern times, the wish for 'the Jews' to be uniquely guilty has led to responsibility for the Holocaust itself being foisted on its victims and, in particular, on Zionists. One version, solemnly propounded in post-war, neo-Nazi circles, maintained that the Gestapo had been run by Jews, and that Hitler was deliberately kept uninformed about what was being done in his name. The Jews could then be said not only to have massacred themselves, but then to have profited from their lies about the German people by claiming damages for something that never happened. Holocaust deniers claim that 'only' some 360,000 Jews died in the camps, where, it is claimed, there were never any gas chambers or systematic killings. Eyewitnesses are, in this case, all deemed to be liars, despite the mass of confirmatory evidence, both documentary and photographic.[36]

In *The Authentic Gospel of Jesus* (2004), the Hebrew scholar Géza Vermès established, with chapter and verse, that the message and the style of Jesus are of a piece with Jewish texts and ideas current in the first half of the first century CE. If Jesus preached an adjacent message, it is a small surprise; the Talmud itself is a compendium of

---

36 See *Eichmann before Jerusalem* (2014) by Bettina Stangneth, *passim*.

marginal opinions and glosses. The theatrical Judaism practised in Herod's Second Temple was detested by the contemporary Essenes, who formed hermetic, 'puritanical' communities in the desert. The more worldly, but doctrinally minimalist, Sadducees rejected the notion of resurrection, and doubted the existence of an afterlife. Pharisaic sophistication, with its Hellenic flavour, argued for some kind of immortality, and decorated the Torah with ingenious glosses. No monotheism is as monolithic as it seems from a distance, Judaism least of all.

In line with what Sigmund Freud would call 'the narcissism of small differences', the authors of the Gospels were at pains to postulate radical hostility between Jesus and the Pharisees – a major source of His ideas. The Christian Fathers were eager to detach Jesus and His 'Church' – a term without sense for the historical figure on whom the apostles constructed their Saviour – from Jewish origins. The Church could then sanctify the incorporation of Yahweh[37] in the Trinity, and of the priesthood into the sole agents of redemption.

---

37 This assimilation prompts the thought of Jesus applying for membership of a smart golf club and being obliged to supply the 'name of father, if changed'. Yahweh, commonly written as Jehovah, is a transcription of the (vowel-free) Hebrew tetragram YHWH, the designations of a God whose name it was impious to say aloud.

St Paul himself never denied the primordial role of Judaism, which ran on, admitted or not, through centuries of persecution. In 1942, in fascist Rome, the German Jesuit Peter Browe wrote of the 'manifest failure of the Christian mission to convert the Jews'. Having set out reasons for the impasse from both sides, Browe then comes to 'the reasons from God's side' and dares to guess that, 'perhaps in the end, God Himself did not want Judaism to be obliterated'. As some Jews have been known to say, 'now He tells us'.

※　※　※

9

IN *JUDAS* (2009), Susan Gubar quotes Karl Barth, a famous modern (anti-Nazi) theologian: 'Like Esau, the rejected of God, [the Jews] sold their birthright for a mess of pottage. They did so not with closed eyes but with open eyes. Yet these were obviously the eyes of the blind … Israel always tried to buy off Yahweh with thirty pieces of silver.' This is brave talk from a Swiss. It is worth noting her use of the word 'always' to endorse the age-old notion of 'the eternal Jew'.

During the Third Reich, Switzerland was willing to give shelter to the silver, but not to its owners. Having provided a haven for legitimate Jewish fortunes, Swiss banks found ways of preventing the heirs of those murdered in the Holocaust from gaining access to their families' money on the grounds that they did not know the passwords. Having profited from these 'deposits' for many decades, Swiss bankers affected outrage at Jewish 'greed' when the United States, in particular, made effective moves to have the money returned, with interest (wouldn't you know it?), to its rightful owners.

Barth's superciliousness was a refinement of Martin Luther's scatological rant.[38] It takes a lofty place in the blaring file of Christian denunciations of the only people to whom Jesus actually chose to address himself (he is reported, credibly, to have been parochial enough to warn his disciples against even going into the cities of Samaria). Judas is seen by Susan Gubar as 'the principal figure through whom Christians have understood Jews and Jewry' – a per-

---

38 Luther was more genial at first, when he hoped to recruit the Jews to his version of Christianity. Once rejected, he grew obscenely abusive; but then he suffered agonisingly from piles – an affliction traditionally associated with Jews.

ennial scoundrel resurrected and scarified, by malicious fancy, from a shadowy, perhaps blameless original.[39]

Judas the Betrayer becomes the enabling hate figure in a myth that requires an innocent victim God, whose blood will redeem those who put their faith in Him. Judas provides the despicable, protean 'other', who can change everything except his spots. Sometimes black, sometimes feminised, he remains essentially 'Jewy'. Yet even the Gospels, written in Greek for a largely Gentile audience, use only a mild word (*paradidomi* means 'I hand/give over') to describe whatever Judas is said to have done to betray Jesus. How much finger-pointing was needed in order to indicate to the authorities a man who had, a day or two earlier, drawn conspicuous attention to himself?

The Jew as intrinsically treacherous is struck from the Judas mould. Alfred Dreyfus was condemned for no better reason. The Nazis found it easy to persuade themselves, and others, that they had lost the Great War only because 'the Jews', having dodged the column, stabbed the

---

39 In *King Jesus* (1946), Robert Graves postulated a Judas who was an eager Zealot, i.e. a true revolutionary against Rome. That Jesus 'loved' him became an embarrassment. To cast him as deceiver and traitor rendered Jesus innocent of complicity and undeserving of Roman condemnation.

fatherland in the back. In truth, 11,000 Jews (a statistically 'disproportionate' number) died fighting for the Kaiser. Reinhard Heydrich and Adolf Eichmann had the grim grace to allow surviving Jewish veterans with medals for gallantry to travel first class (at their own expense) on the trains carrying them to the death camps.

Christian rhetoric processed raw history through theological parable into ideological scheme. Judas doubled with the Eternal Jew as the emblematic perennial scoundrel. Sedulous scholars were quick to find choice passages that might be said to show that, even before the advent of Christ, Jews were regarded with revulsion by pagan Greeks and Romans. They were indeed often depicted, notably by the aristocratic Roman historian Tacitus, as absurd and perverse outsiders; but the same was true of almost all foreigners as soon as historians began to fabricate stories that flattered their audiences. Tacitus spoke well of the Germans, whose tribesmen destroyed Quintilius Varus's three legions in 9 CE, principally in order to contrast their beery virility with contemporary Roman decadence. In *A Most Dangerous Book* (2011), Christopher Krebs takes accurate pleasure in showing how the Nazis preened themselves by lending 'Gospel' significance to Tacitus's straight-faced ironies. In the same way, national socialism appropriated Nietzsche's notion of the blond superman to make him its patron philosopher. In several places, however, Nietzsche chose to proclaim the moral superiority of the Jews to the Germans. In the Tacitean style, perhaps, it amused him to pique his countrymen (and Richard Wagner) by promoting their supposed 'other'.

Among Greeks and Romans, mutual abuse and the detection of unspeakable habits in each other and in 'barbarians' of one kind or another was widespread. How many neighbours in the ancient or the modern world are found to love each other? Polytheism, however, had no uniform ideology or coercive mission. The great Hellenist Arnaldo Momigliano said that he had studied Greek religion for fifty years and, at the end of them, he still did not know exactly what the Greeks expected of their gods or the gods of the Greeks.

There was a small foretaste of the intolerance of ideologues when Hippasos of Metapontum, a brilliant fifth-century BCE disciple of Pythagoras, was expelled from the party, as it were, and possibly done to death by other members of the sect for doctrinal eccentricity.

Christianity was the first religion to demand universal obedience to dogma and to require subservience, on pain of death, to those who preached it.[40] The notion of heresy lent virtue to hierarchy.

Until the early second millennium CE, Jewish scholars and books continued to receive respect from at least some Christian divines, the 'liberal' Christian intellectual Peter Abélard among them. The discovery of his illicit love affair with Héloïse d'Argenteuil was made into a pretext for hardening the 'discipline', and narrowing the horizon, of the Church. Abélard was castrated and Héloise locked away in a convent. In 1209, Pope Innocent III turned intolerance into a battle cry, when those fighting Albigensian heretics found it difficult to distinguish them from honest Catholics: 'Kill them all,' said the Vicar of Christ, *'novit enim Dominus qui sunt ejus'* (God would sort out which was which). It is tempting to guess that there was a certain shortening of the Christian temper when the Second Coming failed to honour the human calendar and make a punctual appearance at the millennium.

---

40 Charles Freeman's 2004 book entitles this new intolerance 'the closing of the western mind'.

The Holocaust or *Shoah* – as Claude Lanzmann chose to call it in his nine-hour documentary film – disconcerted the complacent vision of God working His purpose out – at least for a time. After Auschwitz, Marc Chagall dared to depict Judas the Jew as the iconic crucified man. The subsequent erection, by the Polish Catholic primate, of a Christian cross in the shadow of the gas chambers, can be read – as can Mel Gibson's sado-masochistic, big-earning film, *The Passion of the Christ* – as an attempt to reappropriate innocent suffering as a Christian monopoly. While in custody for drunk-driving, Gibson let it be known that Jews were responsible for all the wars in the world. The unasked question loiters over post-war Christendom: if 'the Jews' are not guilty, who is?

First represented as a duplicitous money-grubber, leaking sexual and faecal abomination, Judas was later transformed into an existential hero, somewhat like the Sisyphus of Albert Camus's myth. René Girard has argued that the mythic Judas mutates from being 'the most wanted man' in a list of archetypical criminals to being 'the one wanted most' – a kind of sacred deliverer, because capable of assuming so much of humanity's guilt. Finally, he emerges as the victim of God's injustice, since – even if he did indeed finger Jesus – he did only what the Christian myth required of him.

*   *   *

10

GREEKS AND ROMANS despised and killed all sorts of people, including each other, in large numbers and for many greedy reasons,[41] without incurring the bloody, predatory reputation of the Jews. Jews were not *that* different until one of them was said (if never by Himself) to be the Son of God. After the fall of Jerusalem in 70 CE and the coincidental obliteration of the 'Jerusalem Church', led by James the brother of Jesus (who both cherished the cult of his brother and continued to honour all the old Jewish practices), Christianity's rise and the dejection of Jews and

---

41 Julius Caesar's conquest of Gaul, undertaken in pursuit both of glory and of enough gold to pay off his bankers, led to the deaths of about a million 'tribesmen' with whom he had no quarrel, although their ancestors had indeed attacked and captured Rome – briefly – some three centuries earlier. Caesar dispensed with the luxury of moral justification for attaching their territory to the Roman Empire.

Judaism went together. Despite copious evidence to the contrary,[42] modern Christian apologists like to claim that the doctrine of anti-Semitism (and the incidental pleasure of principled persecution) is a feature not of Christianity, but of the Enlightenment.

It was, however, after witnessing the savage war between sixteenth-century Catholics and Protestants that Michel de Montaigne remarked that a man must be very sure of himself if he can condemn another to be roasted alive. This lack of rigour earned his work a place on the Vatican's index of forbidden books. Punctual pundits find it worth mentioning that Montaigne's (Catholic) mother was of Spanish *marrano* origin. In theological reckoning, beliefs are sacred and escape the call for 'psychological' or genetic explanation.

In the recycling of prejudice, there is no lack of philosophers. Voltaire, Kant, Hegel and Marx made 'the Jews' the indigestible 'other' in history and in ideal societies, for which they supplied a range of purgative *a priori* recipes. Although he never said so out loud, the contamination of philosophy by religion may have something to do with the young Ludwig Wittgenstein's announcement that his

---

42 Some of it is set out, readably, in Malcolm Hay's *Thy Brother's Blood: The Roots of Christian Anti-Semitism* (1975), Malcolm Hay was a Roman Catholic.

object in philosophy was to 'show the fly the way out of the fly-bottle'. Meanwhile, the beliefs traditionally classed as 'metaphysics' could best be rendered superfluous to modern life by not being talked about at all. 'Whereof one cannot speak, thereof one should keep silent' stands as the Biblical-style translation of the last words of Wittgenstein's *Tractatus Logico-Philosophicus* (1921) – a title deliberately parodic of Spinoza's masterwork *Tractatus Theologico-Politicus*.

Spinoza's break with Judaism has been taken to be an emancipatory element in what Jonathan Israel called 'the radical Enlightenment'. Spinoza did indeed say harsh things about Judaism; but it demands no rare squint to see that what he dared openly to question in the faith of his fathers was equally questionable, *mutatis mutandis*, in the Christianity about which he chose to be reticent. Despite his rejection of ancestral allegiance, Spinoza continued to be called 'the Jew', even by his philosophical admirer and rival Gottfried Wilhelm Leibniz.

When the Nazis came to power, Martin Heidegger, a one-time Catholic seminarian, was prompt to speak of his erstwhile university colleagues as 'the Jew X' or 'the Jew Y'. Although a prompt post-war advocate of Jewish emancipation from guilt, Jean-Paul Sartre had had no hesitation in taking the place of a dismissed Jewish *lycée* professor in 1940. When, in 'Anti-Semite and Jew' (1946), Sartre advised surviving Jews to embrace their distinction, he knew little about Jewish history, more about the symbolic place of 'the Jews' in the *a priori* political logics[43] in which French intellectuals specialise. For an idea to be valid, it must be universally applicable. Peculiarity is always obnoxious; and who is more peculiar than 'the Jew'? When it came to the anti-Semite, Sartre typified him as the man who – facing himself with the question, 'who am I?' – is able to say, 'I am someone who hates Jews', and then, having put in his moral dentures, can snarl at the world.

With his penchant for having things both ways, Sartre both 'legitimised' Palestinian terrorism and endorsed the existence of Israel. He remained uneasy about Jewish particularism, until, late in life, he fell under the influence of

---

43 The common aspect of such logics is that you determine their categorical terms ahead of time and then draw syllogistic conclusions. For a simple example, capitalism (or killing God) is wicked, Jews are typical capitalists (or deicides), therefore Jews are wicked. Anti-Semites often have no personal experience of Jews and fail to recognise them when they meet them. For a poignant example, see Daniel Cordier's *Alias Caracalla* (2009), an autobiography in which the very young French Resistance recruit meets the great political writer Raymond Aron in Gaullist circles in London. Aron is wise, gentle and not at all patronising. When Cordier, who had been a youthful activist in Maurras's *Action Française*, was told that Aron was a Jew, he could not believe it. His preconceived conception of the world was permanently punctured. He became an art dealer.

the then Maoist Benny Lévy, who became his secretary and persuaded him that he was some kind of a Jew. Lévy was later accused by Simone de Beauvoir, Sartre's consort *depuis toujours*, of the *détournement d'un vieillard* (the misleading of an old man). After Sartre's death, Lévy went to Israel and dedicated himself to Jewish studies.

In today's Britain, a posse of high-minded university teachers has announced the boycott of visiting Israeli academics. One need not be a cynic of rare doggedness to guess that, if anyone who could be accused of 'Zionism' were to be relieved of his or her job, there would be no shortage of worthy applicants. In the same spirit of ostentatious nobility, in 2015, 500 British creative persons signed a letter to *The Guardian*, declaring that they will not, under any circumstances, accept any prizes or awards from Israeli sources. It may be doubted whether Ken Loach or Mike Leigh is a keen reader of the Duke de la Rochefoucauld, but each deserves to be saddled with the ducal dictum: 'Whoever refuses praise asks to be praised twice.'

Some twenty years ago, Ken Loach directed a play at the Royal Court Theatre that proclaimed the Zionists 'collaborated' with the Nazis in order to get German Jews to migrate to Palestine. This was a wilful distortion of what was, in

fact, a negotiation to save at least some Jews from the fate
that was coming to them, not least because the nations of
the world had turned their backs on them, as was proved by
the Évian Conference in 1938. Loach is adept at the tendentious representation of historical events — for instance, the
Spanish Civil War, in the service of a Manichaean ideology,
in which it is a preconceived item of faith that 'nationalism' is a bourgeois abomination. Hence, while, in theory,
it is wrong for fascism to persecute Jews, it is, at the same
time, illicit for Jews to have a specific, national ambition
and political identity.[44]

Wittgenstein's very rich Viennese family converted
to Catholicism, but he came to confess that he was, in
truth, three-quarters Jewish. If his philosophy was a sublime expression of the desire to show Jews the way out of
their penitential isolation, he lived through the Holocaust
without making any louder allusion to it than did most of
the English intelligentsia. The Jews of Europe were murdered, not only because the Nazis and their auxiliaries were
keen to kill (and dispossess) them, but also because the

---

44 The late Alan Sillitoe, working-class author of *Saturday Night and Sunday Morning*,
became an ardent supporter of Zionism after hearing a number of left-wing friends
gloating over the death of Israeli children in a terrorist attack.

exterminators could assume, with justice, that no one would take measures to stop them.

In one of the essays in *Why I Am Not a Christian* (1927), the great liberal philosopher Bertrand Russell declared that, if it could be proved that killing all the Jews in the world would procure an earthly paradise for the rest of the human race, there was no logical reason not to proceed to their annihilation. Russell was quick to say that, in practice, no such proof could possibly be valid, but his *jeu d'esprit* served to show to what degree, despite the title of his collection, he actually *was* a Christian. Did Russell seriously suppose that, if a divine edict promised mankind a blissful future were all the Jews in the world to be killed, this would supply an *ethical* dispensation for their murderers? It calls for little Talmudic resource to see that, as the story of Abraham and Isaac implies, such a promise would be a *temptation* not a deliverance.

To kill Jews has been a time-honoured prescription for keeping people together when societies begin to fall apart. Today's ruction within the European Union coincides with nostalgic recourse to the myth of a Jewish conspiracy. If Israel cannot easily be destroyed, because of its 'illicit' capacity to defend itself with nuclear weapons, it can and must be vilified, and, in a world-political sense, ghettoised. Religious anti-Judaism had a political successor in 'ethnic' anti-Semitism; anti-Semitism in anti-Zionism. This righteous sentiment permits affectations of 'innocence' from racial prejudice in, for loud instance, Tom Paulin despite his poetic wish literally to shoot Jewish 'settlers'.[45] Zionists have become the target of choice for those who expect to be covered in glory by casting the first stone. Is there any other category of person of which an Oxford don, or any civilised person, would care to boast a willingness to kill on sight?

*　　*　　*

11

ON 7 JANUARY 2015, two French-born and French-educated brothers, Said and Chérif Kouachi, forced their way into the Paris offices of the satirical magazine

---

45 That Paulin is himself a son of Ulster's 'Ascendancy', composed of the descendants of Protestant colonists, could be said to suggest an element of Oedipal apology in his murderous ambition.

Charlie Hebdo and shot to death eleven innocent people. Eleven more people were injured. As the murderers
headed for their getaway car, an already wounded French
policeman, who happened to be a Muslim, was shot, at
close range, as he held up his hands. On the same day, at
much the same time, four customers in a kosher supermarket in a Parisian suburb were murdered by another
'commando' of Islamic militants. A number of customers
were herded to safety, in a cold store, by a Muslim supermarket employee. That the gunmen were French-born is
a very small paradox. It is no wild speculation to suspect
that the notion that they should be grateful for reluctant
mercies struck them as Uncle Tomfoolery. Sartre's notion,
expressed in his introduction to Frantz Fanon's *Les Dam-
nés de la terre* (1961), that a man liberates himself into true
manhood by killing a (colonialist) oppressor has come
home to roost. Philosophy, too, has its poisoned wells.

A long article in the *Sunday Times* of 25 January 2015,
by the historian and French specialist Robert Tombs,
treated the *Charlie Hebdo* massacre with academic
superbe. While deploring the killings, Tombs thought
it right to say that the cartoons in which the magazine
lampooned the Prophet Muhammad were deliberately

provocative. 'Baiting' Muslims was a socially divisive and dangerous game and, while on the one hand, freedom of expression might be a precious democratic right, there was also the other hand, which touted the message[46] that French intellectuals would be prudent and to alienating their scorn for Islam. To rupture its immunity from criticism would cause unnecessary offence and might lead to more sectarian violence.

After long politico-religious ructions during the 1880s and 1890s, the French made it an essential characteristic of the Third Republic that citizens, while entitled to worship as they pleased, must not impose their views on others. In the nationwide educational curriculum, devised in the 1880s by the Freemason Jules Ferry, time was allowed, out of school on Wednesday afternoons, for religious instruction. Formally, France became a *société laïque*, independent of clerical domination. On Tombs's reckoning, tact now demands that Muhammad be regarded as the only human being immune from criticism and from any but deferential portrayal. Radical Islamic intimidation is so dangerous

---

46 By writing at length in the *Sunday Times* (circulation two million) about what had appeared in a magazine that sold no more than 60,000 copies, Tombs was giving publicity to the 'baiting' he deplored. Presumptions of moral perfect pitch allowed him to take Rupert Murdoch's shillings by baiting the *bien-pensants*.

that the French should abandon iconoclastic skittishness and defer to imminent *force majoritaire*. Meanwhile, we are tipped the wink that it would be prudent to return to the intimidated quietism that Marshal Pétain's Vichy had imposed under the German occupation. If the Republic, based on secular values, had become upsetting to fanatics, it should surrender its licence.

In *Lettres Persanes* (1721), Montesquieu ironises left and right. In letter 24, Rica (one of his alien correspondents) reports how there is a great magician in the West who can make people believe that three is one, that the bread we eat is not bread, and the wine not wine, plus *'mille autres choses de cette espèce'* (a thousand other things of this order). Mordant levity is part of civilised intelligence. In the words of Jacques Roger, Montesquieu testifies that *'la seule faute impardonnable aux philosophes qui pensent juste, c'est d'être ennuyeux'* (the only unpardonable fault in philosophers who think rightly is to be boring). Professor Tombs gives the impression that writers can be boring, as long as they are not provocative. General de Gaulle, *à propos* the revolutionary rhetoric of Sartre, said 'one does not put Voltaire in jail'. The new wisdom would leave him free to speak, as long as he did not remove his gag.

In less skittish mood, Montesquieu was magisterial when, in 1720, he dismissed the old Christ-killer image of the Jew: 'The Jewish religion is an old trunk that has produced two branches that have covered the entire earth: Muhammadanism and Christianity ... It is a mother who has given birth to two daughters who have covered her with a thousand plagues.'[47] The comedy, of a kind, is that both these daughters have advertised their ambition for the more-or-less enforced universal conversion of humanity, while both accuse 'the Jews' of a conspiracy to take command of the world.

One of the side-effects of the French Revolution was the admission of French Jews to citizenship, on condition that they renounce their status as any kind of distinct people. The formula devised by Count Stanislas de Clermont-Tonnerre in 1789 allowed Jews, as individuals, all the privileges of citizenship, but no respectable place or legal status to 'the Jews as a people'. Clermont-Tonnerre's offer was largely accepted and honoured. It contrasted with Voltaire's earlier stigmatisation of 'the Jews' as vessels of avaricious evil, quite as if less than 0.5 per cent

---

47 Cited by Michael Goldfarb, *Emancipation* (2009).

of the population could represent a rampant threat to society.

Voltaire adduced no evidence of Jewish iniquity, but was able to be specific in denouncing Catholic vindictiveness. It was typified by the Calas affair, in which an innocent Protestant was broken on the wheel in 1762, supposedly for murdering a son who had wanted to convert to Catholicism. Voltaire's determination *écraser l'infâme* did not extend to the Vatican's diabolisation of Jews, from which he did not at all dissent. As any ironist might hope, Voltaire was renowned for his avarice, and eager to make profitable financial deals. In all but confession, he impersonated the kind of Jew he thought so reprehensible.

In *Splendeurs et misères des courtisanes*, written in the 1840s, the entertaining Honoré de Balzac referred to the '*race maudite*', from whom Esther, his heroine, is a beautiful apostate. Balzac's protracted mockery of the tortured French accent of her sugar daddy, the plutocratic Baron Nucingen, supplies an early instance of the demonisation that made it credible that 'the Jews' were archetypal capitalist swindlers. They remained fat targets for French brickbats.

At the time of the Dreyfus affair, the many readers

of Edouard Drumont's *La France juive* seemed to agree with him that their country was in thrall to its very small, almost invariably law-abiding Jewish population. At the end of the affair, the unforgivable crime of Alfred Dreyfus was that, after all the convulsions and divisions his conviction had caused, the 'traitor' was proved to be entirely innocent. A broad strand of French opinion could never forgive 'the Jew', in particular and in general, for not being the desired duplicitous monster. Louis-Ferdinand Céline's polemic novel *Bagatelles pour un massacre* (1937) was an overt prescription (Céline was a doctor) for the mass murder of Jews. The author's admiration for the Nazis led to his temporary exile after the war, but, in 1951, he returned to France and literary fame. Not even his bitterest critics ever proposed that Céline's books be censored because they 'baited' Jews. Both Bernard-Henri Lévy and George Steiner have celebrated his genius.

Distaste for Jews may have been endemic in France but, until the accession of Philippe Pétain in 1940, it was not legitimised as it was in Hungary (as early as 1920, by the introduction of the *numerus clausus* in all the professions). Charles Maurras demanded that Léon Blum – Prime Minister of France's popular front – should be shot, '*dans le dos*'. Blum was severely injured when a bunch of louts took their cue from Maurras and attacked his car. Maurras was so reckless in his parade of ultramontane intolerance (and so literally deaf to criticism) that he was excommunicated. This did not greatly affect his readership in right-wing Catholic circles. Although a fervent anti-German nationalist, he described the French capitulation in 1940, and the consequent dismantling of the Third Republic, as a 'divine surprise'. When Philippe Pétain sanctioned the deportation to the death camps of a quarter of France's Jews, and of all the foreign Jews whom the French police could root out, Maurras's newspaper, *Action française*, printed addresses where candidates for extinction could be located. Pétain's Prime Minister Pierre Laval announced that Jewish children should be transported along with their parents. Such was the sense of family in the clerically dominated *État français*.

In 1989, following the publication of his novel *The Satanic Verses*, Salman Rushdie went in fear of his life after the Ayatollah Khomeini issued a *fatwa* (in this case, a sentence of death) against him. Not a few western intellectuals, Hugh Trevor-Roper among them, deplored

Rushdie's blasphemous cheek rather more than the Ayatollah's want of a sense of humour.[48] Michel Houellebecq's
2015 novel *Soumission* – in which a certain tranche of
French politicians is depicted as acquiescing in a Muslim
France – has been similarly regarded as wantonly, and,
as the cant would say, unhelpfully, inflammatory. It fea-
tures a nice Muslim, brought to presidential power in 2022
with the connivance of the left (what's left of it). Houellebecq's wicked augury (he foresaw the gunshots in Paris)
makes it more likely that Marine Le Pen, the articulate
leaderene of the quasi-fascist Front National, will have a
good chance of reaching the last stage of the presidential
election in 2017.

Since their arrival in the 1960s, many Muslim immigrants from the Maghreb, although French citizens, have
been denied opportunities for upward mobility in an
increasingly stagnant French economy. Their frustration
may well have encouraged fantasies of an Arab hegemony
of the kind that was aborted at the Battle of Tours in 732
CE, when the Moorish invaders of Europe were driven

---

48 Might it be that Trevor-Roper and other refined persons were so very displeased with
Rushdie because the troublemaker was alien to civility and ought not to have made
demands for protection from people among whom he was lucky enough to find himself treated as an equal?

back beyond the Pyrenees. The existence of Israel supplies a 'moral' justification for shooting schoolchildren in Toulouse or beating up, kidnapping, torturing and murdering individual Jews in the unpoliced streets of the Parisian *banlieues*. French Muslim hostility to Jews was countersigned by the Vichy-style anti-Semitism flaunted by the founder of the Front National, Jean-Marie Le Pen. It may be symptomatic of altered attitudes in France's non-Muslim population that Marine Le Pen has split publicly with her father Jean-Marie on the Jewish issue.

If the new anti-Semitism no longer appeals to all tastes, it is a European tradition to resolve internal rifts by common recourse to beating on the killers of Christ. In the 1380s, civil discord inside Paris was resolved with the cry '*aux Juifs*', and the consequent pillage and massacre of the Jewish quarter,[49] although the contentious issue, in which Jews played no part, was between the citizens and the Crown. A century earlier, the French King Louis IX was hailed as 'Saint Louis' after he endorsed Pope Innocent III's 'Albigensian Crusade' and furthered the universal imposition of Christianity by burning the Talmud and

49 See Volume III of Jonathan Sumption's *The Hundred Years' War* (2009).

going to the Holy Land, where his piety did nothing to save him from humiliation, capture and imprisonment. He returned, eventually, to France, chastened, but in no way disposed to abandon his single-minded faith or the stringency of its enforcement on others

* * *

12

ROBERT TOMBS'S FAILURE to mention the Paris supermarket killing of Jews implied, intentionally or not (the latter alternative is at once more innocent and more sinister), that while the *Charlie Hebdo* murders were significant because of the demographic threat of France's six million and counting Muslim inhabitants, shooting Jews could be relegated to a *fait divers*. The fact that the killers were French-born was the most alarming, and embarrassing, aspect of the shooting in the rue Nicolas-Appert. It was a reminder both of the national humiliation of a lost empire and of how many French-born Muslims now constitute the French 'Palestinians', *mais il faut pas le dire.* While their religion bonds and brands them, they and their progeny have the vote. Now about 10 per cent of the population, they could be determinant in a future election. By comparison, it seems that the misgivings or misfortunes of French Jews are of negligible consequence: there are not enough of them to merit appeasement.[50] The morality of contemporary societies is based on economics, not on values.

Here is Tombs's summing-up of the situation in today's France:

> To identify with *Charlie Hebdo* as the torchbearer of freedom is … to identify with this republican vision [of 'republican values' mentioned earlier]. The murder of the cartoonists has been alarmingly successful in terms of the terrorists' presumed aims of deepening and dramatising existing divisions. *Charlie Hebdo*'s secularism, extraordinarily brave in the light of threats of arson and murder, nevertheless seems part of France's problem rather than its

---

50 There are said to be 600,000 Jews in France, but the ones in greatest danger (and likeliest to emigrate) tend to be *petits bourgeois,* with little choice but to live adjacent to Muslims in dangerous locations. The *haute juiverie* is unlikely to have the same anxieties. What Sartre called 'serialisation' discourages overt Jewish solidarity, except among intellectuals.

solution. Rather than forcing fundamentalists to be free, it
has furnished them with further grievances.

The presumption is that the terrorists' purpose was, in
some regard, rational. What is made to follow from it
depends on ignoring the killers' announced reason for
the outrage, which was to 'avenge the Prophet'. Tombs
makes it seem that *Charlie Hebdo*'s outrageousness – its
raison d'être – provoked the murder of its staff and was,
on that account, part of France's 'problem'. Secularism
(here attached to *Charlie Hebdo* but paraded as a general
idea) is first accused of coercion – to what end? – and then
deemed the generator of Muslim grievances.

Is there any evidence that terrorism would not exist if
secularists (i.e. believers in an 'open society', but not necessarily enemies of God or religion) were to abate their
enthusiasm for pluralism? Will Muslims be disposed, in
any large numbers, to abandon their claims to be the only
soldiers of the true God? Will any who veer towards secularism have confidence that their apostasy will not, as the
Quran stipulates, warrant their execution? Who are we to
tell people that their faith is misguided? (Then again, in
a free society, who do you have to be?) The underlying

argument seems to be that liberal culture, which allows religious views but seeks, or sought, to propagate secular values, has become an affront to certain people and should therefore lose its licence.

❊   ❊   ❊

13

IN THE TENTH century CE, Salerno, south of Naples in Italy, was the first practical medical school in Europe. According to legend, the Jew Helinus, the Greek Pontus, the Arab Adela and the Latin Salernus were co-founders of a school unequalled in fame for three centuries. It possessed a unique library of Greek and Arabic texts, taken from the adjacent monastery of Montecassino. Medicine promoted a therapeutic neutrality beyond the scope of any revealed religion. Since medieval medicine was largely a matter of prescribing herbal remedies, combined with a soothing or impressive bedside manner, its non-denominational practice rarely did much harm.

When the plague known as the Black Death more than decimated thirteenth-century Europe, neither physic nor prayers could allay its course. How did good Christians come to be subject to such an agonising and implacable fate? No loving God could visit them with such horrors. The only plausible explanation was that some furtive and malevolent agency was at work. If, as tradition promised, some Jews were capable of effecting 'miraculous' cures (they were often the medical advisers of kings and sultans), it was plausible to suppose that they were equally capable of generating spiteful contagions.

The fourteenth-century French poet Guillaume de Machaut, in his *Judgement of the King of Navarre*, gave what purported to be an eyewitness account of the terror. There were signs in the heavens; stones rained down and killed people; whole towns were struck by lightning and many died. Some of the deaths were due, the poet claims, to the malevolence of the Jews and their Christian accomplices, who poisoned the rivers. The slow grind of heavenly justice eventually put things right by revealing the malefactors to the rest of the population, who massacred all of them. All the same, people continued to die, in ever greater numbers, until one day, when Guillaume heard music in the street and the sound of men and women laughing.

The Protestant René Girard points out in *Le Bouc émis-saire* (1982) – his study of what he calls the 'scapegoat mechanism' – that honest critics ever since the sixteenth century have been sceptical of the specific accusations made against 'the Jews', but the tone of Guillaume's verses rings on down the ages with a sound very like the warning bell once carried by lepers:

After this, came a shittiness,
False, treacherous and defiant,
That was Jewry, the contemptible,
The wicked, the disloyal,
Which is and loves all evil things,
That yielded them much gold and silver,
Then rivers and springs,
That had been clear and healthy,
Poisoned in many places,
Which ended many lives;

But heaven, sitting high and seeing far,
That governs all and all provides,

Quickly forbade this treason
And made it so generally known,
That (Jewry) lost their lives and goods.
For every Jew was destroyed,
Some hanged, others roasted,
Some drowned, others decapitated
By axe or sword.[51]

Medieval communities so dreaded the plague that its mere mention created alarm. People chose not to speak of it or even take measures against it, lest it make things worse. Their only recourse was to find a scapegoat and vent communal dread and hatred on the selected victims. It hardly needs to be said, but had better be, that no Jew was ever shown actually to have done anything to poison a river or a well, nor was any Jew ever proved to have abducted a Christian child and used its blood to make Passover *matzo.* In truth, Jews have always had a horror of consuming blood of any kind. Their ritual slaughter of suitable animals was designed specifically to bleed them before they could be cooked.

---

51 Translated by FR.

Matzo is unleavened bread, the only kind the ancient Hebrews had time to make before they fled from slavery in Egypt. It may be that simple souls confused it with the Christian 'host', which supposedly is one with the body of Christ. Jews were also accused of stealing the sacred wafer and abusing it until it bled. Might it be that the need for them to be guilty owed something to an apprehension that they were, in truth, innocent? With grim glee, George Steiner has suggested that the deep grudge against the Jews is not their failure to embrace the gospel of love, but rather that a demanding revision of their God, and an alien morality, has been imposed on Europe by the Semite Jesus, while the rest of his tribe stand outside its guilt-making creed. Might anti-Semitism also be an expression of resentment at being saddled with Christianity?

*   *   *

14

IN THE WESTERN Pyrenees, where Basque is the common language, a social group known as *Cagots* or

Agotes, who are said to be descended from Germanic or
Visigothic aliens, or from lepers, were rejected with con-
tumely by other Basques for almost a thousand years or
so. They still tend to live in closed villages. They are said
to be distinguished by their blue eyes and by having no
lobes to their ears – a deficiency shared with the Duke of
Wellington and Lord Byron. Since they were (and are)
practising Roman Catholics, *Agotes* could not be denied
the sacraments, but, for centuries, they were accorded the
ritual bread and wine through a hole in the church wall
by priests who, it is said, were particularly venomous (for
no declared reason) in their hostility.

Agotes still live in distinct, ghetto-like villages where
they specialised in indoor trades, especially metal-working.
They are still reluctant to be quizzed about their history.[52]
No accessible source explains why they became scapegoats, but their wariness of others no doubt confirmed that
they had something to hide. Like Jews, *Agotes* tended to
be endogamous, not least because, if they tried to marry
other Basque Catholics, they were liable to be killed. They
too were said to suffer from 'self-hatred'. The lack of ear-

---

52 When, in the 1990s, I visited one of their villages, there was no café, nor any shop where
conversation was welcome.

lobes took the place of the absence of foreskins to denote their 'deformed' character.

*   *   *

15

THE NOTION THAT Jewish medicine, of one kind or another, was sometimes benign, sometimes malevolent, persisted into modern times. In 1953, Joseph Stalin arrested, and would have executed, all the Jewish doctors who had been convoked, because of their rare expertise, to save his life. When they proved incapable of procuring immortality for the Kremlin's paranoid tenant, it remained plausible – presumably to large sections of the Soviet public, and certainly to Joseph the Terrible – that clever Jews should be given to duplicity and commerce with the Devil. Medicine still carries a hint of magic, if not necromancy. The careful illegibility and esoteric terminology of medical prescriptions continues to carry a vestige of medieval abracadabra. More naughty than malicious, Vladimir Nabokov, a philo-Semite with a formidable Jewish wife, referred to Sigmund Freud as 'the Viennese witchdoctor'. Joseph Roth, in a letter of 1926, observed 'Jewish doctors are a sort of atonement for the crucifixion'.

In sixteenth-century London, Ruy Lopez, Queen Elizabeth I's *marrano* physician, was executed on suspicion of being a spy: treachery was taken to be the mark of the Jew, not least when he swore that he no longer was one. The Queen herself could not save the *marrano* from the scaffold. As he was publicly disembowelled, the London crowd was amused that he repeatedly screamed that he was as good a Christian as his tormentors. Ever since the expulsion of England's Jews by Edward I in 1290, the London mob had been denied the sadistic pleasures available on the continent. When the King had dispossessed and evicted the Jews, those who owed them money applauded his Christian virtues; but once the usurers were gone, Edward exacted every last penny of what had been owed to them. This did nothing to discourage G. K. Chesterton – English literature's lovable papist – from calling Edward the 'tender father of his people' and a 'knight-errant'.

Shylock is said to have been based on Ruy Lopez. However memorably Shakespeare allowed the baited

Shylock to speak for himself,[53] the London crowd of his day behaved with much greater savagery than the Venetians, whom Shakespeare was pleased to satirise. While Jews were still formally banned from entering England, the Serene Republic had the mercantile sense to make Jews somewhat welcome, although they were sequestered in their ghetto where, true to their fractious habits, Sephardim and Ashkenazi had separate synagogues. As a trading republic, Venice was happy to make use of its Jewish inhabitants. By unsurprising coincidence, when England became the Cromwellian republic, the Protector allowed useful Jews to return, quietly. Puritans had a certain affinity with the Jews: they too regarded themselves as divinely 'chosen'.

Some scholars claim that Shakespeare may well have had first-hand experience of Jews. A small number of *marranos* were his neighbours in Elizabethan London. It is more likely that Shylock was based on the folkloric figure of the avaricious Jew counting furtive shekels in

---

53 In his *Shylock* (1993), John Gross is confident that Shylock was conceived as a scoundrel and a butt for audience derision and was played as such until Sir Henry Irving, in particular, played him for pathos. Thanks to Shakespeare's genius for impersonation, the part proved to have enough elasticity to be played, movingly, against his presumed intentions.

some dank, dark room (Dickens's Fagin came from the same stock-pot).[54] Shakespeare's genius is more likely than fieldwork to have led him to transcend the stereotype. The dramatist has to impersonate his characters; that is where he finds the sympathy, however reluctant, which logic disdains.

✳   ✳   ✳

16

JEW-BAITING JOINS UP the dottiness in a number of the greatest English literary talents. Only George Eliot's *Daniel Deronda* and Benjamin Disraeli's fictional advertisements for himself buck the trend. Chaucer's *Prioress's Tale* sanctified the 'blood libel'; Shylock and Fagin supplied maquettes for your 'Yid of all seasons'; the saintly T. S. Eliot provided Bleistein with his cigar and put the jew (*sic*) 'underneath the lot'. Eliot's admirers would have us

---

54 Both Shakespeare and Dickens (the latter more out of embarrassment than conviction) created 'good' Jews; but the public appetite for Jewish villains, and authorial enthusiasm in creating them, means that few people can give a name to the virtuous Hebrews.

understand that he was going through a bad patch, trouble with the first missus and all.

As for that other Edwardian *kulchural* import Ezra Pound, his poetic output is rabid with hate against Jews. Even after the Holocaust, he would still write in 1945 that the '*goyim* are cattle [who] go to saleable slaughter'.[55] If only to avoid being tried for treason by the American authorities, he announced in public that he regretted yielding to the 'suburban prejudice of anti-Semitism'. Business was business: in 1949, he was awarded the Bollingen Prize, the major American literary honour for poetry. Eliot was on the jury and voted for 'Ole Ez', as Pound referred affectionately to himself (Richard Aldington, poet and hero of the Great War, labelled Pound a 'draft-dodger', which he was, twice). Karl Shapiro, a good poet with a brave record in the Second World War, dissented from his fellow Bollingen jurors and was ejected from the literary pantheon. In private, Pound continued to be an unreformed anti-Semite: he was reluctant even to meet people with Jewish-sounding names.

---

55 *Goyim* is a routine term, among some Ashkenazi Jews, for Gentiles, rather as the British used to (and not a few still do) speak of 'foreigners'. The term is used in an understandably unattributed response to the little rhyme: 'How odd / Of God / To choose / The Jews ... Because the *goyim* / Annoy Him.'

Chaucer's fiction popularised the 'blood libel', which claims that Jews kidnap Christian boys and use their blood in the recipes for their Passover *matzos*. Who will be surprised to hear that charges of infanticide and of cannibalism had first been levelled against the early Christians? Chaucer based his story on 'Little Hugh' of Lincoln, whose body was discovered in a well on 29 August 1255. Copin (or Jopin), a local Jew, was denounced and, under torture, confessed to killing the child. He was then executed. About six months earlier, King Henry III had sold his rights to tax the Jews to his brother Richard, Earl of Cornwall. Having lost this source of income, he decreed that if a Jew were convicted of a crime, any money he had would then belong to the King. As a result, some ninety Jews were arrested in connection with Little Hugh's death and charged with ritual murder. Eighteen were hanged for refusing to throw themselves on the mercy of a Christian jury. King Henry expropriated the property of those convicted. The others were pardoned and set free, probably because Richard, fearing a threat to his own source of income, intervened on their behalf. The alleged martyrdom of Little Hugh continued to be honoured with a plaque in Lincoln Cathedral until 1955, when it was removed and replaced with a decorous apology to those who had been falsely accused.

Not a single case of abduction was ever proved, anywhere; no corpse (desiccated or not) was ever uncovered; no confession (except after prolonged torture) was ever extracted; no bloody water-biscuits were found in any Jewish larder. But might that not prove just how clever those people can be at covering their tracks? Imagine how desperately latter-day Chester-Bellocians would have railed against all Jews if as many rabbis had been convicted of habitual paedophilia as have Roman Catholic priests.

The charm of the 'blood libel' persisted into modern times. In 1840, the otherwise cynical French Prime Minister Adolphe Thiers was quick to credit his fat-headed consul in Syria, when he reported that local Jews had kidnapped the Catholic Father Thomas. The British Foreign Secretary Lord Palmerston recalled his legate in Syria – perhaps for noble reasons, but certainly to discredit the French – and denounced the trumped-up charge. For those who relish irony, in 1858 in Bologna, the Holy Inquisition kidnapped a Jewish boy, Edgardo Mortara, from his family home, on the grounds that he had been 'baptised' by an ignorant servant girl, and now belonged to Mother

Church. This had a mutation, sometimes benign, in the baptism of Jewish children in hiding during the *Shoah*. Surviving relatives had difficulty retrieving those who had been 'saved'.

Although the image of the blood-thirsty Jew persists, the last instance of a Jew being charged formally with killing a Christian child and using its blood to make *matzo* took place over a century ago, in Kiev. The Tsarist government arraigned Mendel Beilis and, after two cruel years in prison, he was brought to trial in front of a jury, seven of whom were chosen because they were members of the anti-Semitic Black Hundreds. They had voted seven to five for conviction when one peasant rose to his feet, prayed to the icon and said that he did not want 'this sin on my soul, he's not guilty'. Years later, when Beilis was asked for his outstanding impression of the trial, he answered: 'The Russian Gentiles, who sacrificed themselves for me – there was real heroism, real sacrifice. They knew that by defending me, their careers would be ruined; even their very lives would not be safe. But they persisted because they knew I was innocent.' Two decades later, an ideology that dispensed with juries came to power in Germany: to be a Jew was automatically to deserve the death penalty.

* * *

17

IN SOUTHERN SPAIN, the *convivencia*, which began in the eighth century CE under the benign supremacy of the Umayyad Moors, encouraged the upper echelons of the Muslim, Christian and Jewish population of Al-Andalus (modern Andalucía) to enjoy a common culture. Poetry, music and philosophy lent harmony to tolerance. This concord was ruptured, first by ardent Christians – who insisted on being martyred, despite the Sultan's patient wish that they cease their provocations (pigs' heads were among their favourite projectiles) – and later by the arrival, from Morocco, of the much more aggressive Almohad form of Islam. In their eyes, Iberian Jews were reliable as servants and soldiers of the Sultan. Judaism and Islam were at one in failing to find any sense in the notion of the Trinity.

Meanwhile, in the Catholic north of thirteenth-century Spain, the Jewish apostates Pablo Christiani and Petrus Alfonsi were pious instances of those who deserted their ancient faith and transformed themselves into its evangelising enemies. In 1263, the sage Rabbi Nachmanides was conscripted to take part in a disputation with a Dominican friar in Barcelona. Nachmanides was warned by his friend (and medical patient) King Jaime II of Aragon that he might defend Judaism but that he must never, on pain of death, dispute the veracity of Christianity. The Jew was confined, metaphysically, to 'playing for a draw'. A winning argument was likely to cost him his life. In the case of Nachmanides, even a clever draw put him in danger. Thanks only to Jaime II, he was able to get away before the vindictive Dominicans laid their hands on him. The same monastic order would save a good many Jews as they were being rounded up in Nazi-occupied Italy. It also assisted the post-war flight from 'torture and persecution' of Nazis such as Adolf Eichmann.

In the Christian imagination, the ghetto created a cloche for bogeymen. For the pinched Jews, it was a home from home, albeit airless and menaced by *pogroms*. Norman Cohn shows how repression of the weak generated a fear, among those who crushed them, that the blanched outcasts were plotting revenge with the aid of arcane powers. The ghetto became a pressure-cooker, heated from without by the caustic imagination of the Church. The Jews, with their unintelligible and exclusive rites, had a reputation for recherché powers that accompanied them down the ages: it armed their 'science' with a tincture of diabolical knowledge. The more they were repressed and reviled, the greater the apprehension that they must be planning revenge. This supplied their enemies with a righteous need to make a pre-emptive strike. At the same time, some Jews at least were credited with rare and valuable knowledge. The Nazi expression 'Jewish science' echoes the mixture of scorn and apprehension with which Kabbalistic intelligence was regarded.[56]

Today, the Israelis' capacity to defend themselves with new, clever weapons (the drone and the 'iron dome') is similarly viewed as giving them an unfair advantage. Edward Luttwak has had the nerve to say aloud that the 'disproportion' between Israeli and Arab casualties may have something to do with the accuracy of Israeli fire and the trained procedures of the IDF. So, far from seeking to protect their 'fighters' or their civilian population, Hamas is happy to maximise their casualties to better advertise their victimisation. All their 'fighters' are laid out as innocent

---

56 Jewish thought was said to be typically theoretical and secretive, not openly experimental. Aryan myth made the earth, not the sky, the source of valid ideas. Heinrich Himmler, who never turned a sod, claimed to be a farmer at heart. In fact, Einstein's general theory of relativity was susceptible to specific empirical proof.

civilians as soon as they are dead. When ends trump means, truth is whatever serves the cause.

After the *reconquista* had unified Spain, the population was united in a form of Roman Catholicism that brooked no deviation. While Catalans might still have looked down on those from Castile, all Spaniards prided themselves both on their faith and on their *pura sangre*: no family of proper *hidalgos* could admit to a drop of unchristian blood. The expropriation of Jewish and Muslim property, and the expulsion of its owners, was justified by a fabricated history that denied one vital consequence of the *conviven cia*: the generation of children, legitimate or not, of mixed blood. *Marranos* – ex-Jews who were allowed to stay in Spain because they had converted, more or (more often) less willingly to Catholicism – were regarded with suspicious, sometimes greedy vigilance by the Inquisition. Many did indeed continue to observe the Jewish law within what they hoped was the secrecy of their own homes.

Spanish Inquisitors, and poets such as Lope de Vega, maintained that Jewish males could be detected because they menstruated, and, so the story went, had tails.[57] As

---

57 The Scots said the same of their allies the French in the 1380s, when the latter landed north of the border and failed to bond with the rugged clansmen. So much for the 'Auld Alliance'.

the Devil himself was sometimes seen as having two tails, when imagined as penises, it was feared that they served to give women what – in Sigmund Freud's phrase – they really wanted. The insatiable eroticism of Jews was publicised (and exaggerated) in the Nazi broadsheet *Der Sturmer*, until audience research showed that the allegation made them more attractive to German females. Goebbels was dismayed when, in 1941, Aryan wives demonstrated publicly in Berlin against the deportation of their German Jewish husbands. The order for deportation was rescinded.

The determination to whitewash 'ordinary' German civilians has inhibited any suggestion that they might, or even should, have been more vocal in their rejection of Nazi legislation. The current Archbishop of Canterbury Justin Welby recently went out of his way to sympathise with the thousands of, as he said, 'innocent' Dresdeners who died in the Allied firebomb raid of 14 February 1945. Their ancient city was indeed beautiful; it was also a major railway junction.[58] Its population had seen – or might have seen, if any had cared to look – large consignments

---

58 And, Michael Burleigh has pointed out, a centre for the production of precision optics of the kind used in gun-sights.

of Jews (and others) being marched to the trains that took them to Auschwitz. No one is recorded as having demonstrated against this traffic, although one Dresden resident is said, by Victor Klemperer, to have whispered an encouraging word or two to the Yellow-Starred professor, who had long been a Protestant convert. Klemperer himself was due to report for deportation on the day after the fire-raid that destroyed Gestapo headquarters and its records. As a result of the confusion in the ruined city, he survived the war.

Jews, being, by definition, bloody, are sometimes said to be 'racially' prone to haemorrhoids. Yosef Yerushalmi's *From Spanish Court to Italian Ghetto* (1971) recounts the Spanish Inquisitors' obsession with the idea that male Jews, because unmanned (by circumcision), were given to menstruation. In seventeenth-century Spain, Isaac Cardoso—a *marrano* physician who later escaped to the freedom of the Italian ghettos, where he reverted to Judaism—treated an *alcalde* of the court, Don Juan de Quiñones, for haemorrhoids.[59] Quiñones had used his learning and library to compile a treatise proving that Jews

---

59 Martin Luther also suffered excruciatingly from piles, which may account for his obsessive use of excremental imagery, often at the expense of the Jews.

had tails and were 'subject to menstrual periods and blood, as punishment for the grave sin they committed'. The author's own piles were:

> So huge and great, and accompanied by blood and pain, that they actually seemed tail-like ... I then said to him: 'Your honour must also be liable in the sin of that [Jesus's] death.' ... He began to laugh and said he did not agree with this, for he has been well proved to be a *hidalgo* of La Mancha.

Many Jews who fled from Spain, and, later, from Portugal, found refuge in the Netherlands, where the Christian population, many of them Protestant, had fought a brave battle, physical and spiritual, to emancipate themselves from Catholic Spain. With rare, if wary, grace, the Dutch authorities tolerated the immigrant Jews forming their own communities and building synagogues. In return, the Jews were expected to keep to themselves and not attract attention to their idiosyncratic habits. Tolerance had its repressive consequences: the Amsterdam Jewish authorities formed a petty *Sanhedrin* (the name given to the High Priest's entourage during the days of the Second

Temple in Jerusalem). Their inquisitorial vigilance over their congregations' orthodoxy reflected the Gentiles' watch on them.[60]

When Adolf Hitler set about converting the Jews of Europe into ash, Francisco Franco, the fascist dictator whom Hitler had done much to install, let it be known that refugee Jews of Sephardic (Iberian) origin would be given asylum in Spain. This decision may be taken as an early indication that Franco suspected that Germany was losing the war. Previously, he had had lists compiled of all latter-day *marranos* resident in Spain. There is small doubt that, had the Nazis been victorious, these people of impure blood would have been delivered for extermination. As it was, Franco's measured magnanimity led him to be accused of having Jewish blood himself. After the Battle of Stalingrad, the French anti-Semite (and doctor) Louis-Ferdinand Céline claimed that Germany was losing the war because Adolf Hitler had been replaced, without anyone knowing, by a Jewish dwarf at the head

---

60 In the 1660s, Uriel (Gabriel) da Costa made his way to Holland and returned to Judaism. When he questioned some of its tenets, he was evicted from an Amsterdam synagogue in a very cruel manner. His humiliation, which may well have been witnessed by the young Spinoza, and subsequent isolation led him to shoot himself. The story of da Costa and the Amsterdam community is told in more detail in my *A Jew Among Romans* (2014).

of the Nazi state. Céline is reported[61] to have uttered his diagnosis at a dinner party given by the German ambassador Otto Abetz in occupied Paris. Céline was assumed to be drunk or mad, and escaped sanction.

* * *

18

IN 2012, GERALD Scarfe, the *Sunday Times*'s long-serving cartoonist, published a caricature of the (democratically elected) Israeli Prime Minister, in which 'Bibi' was depicted, with a gloating expression, building the defensive wall – ugly or 'illegal' though it may be – that has served to protect Israeli citizens from suicide bombers. The big giggle of the cartoon was that Netanyahu was depicted using the blood of Palestinian children to cement his wicked bricks. A spicy addition was that Scarfe published his revision of the age-old

---

61 By Ernst Jünger in his memoirs, and by Jacques Benoist-Méchin in *De la défaite au désastre* (1984). Reinhardt Heydrich, architect of the 'Final Solution', was also rumoured, quite falsely, to be half-Jewish.

'blood libel' on Holocaust Remembrance Day. The cartoonist admitted, *du bout des lèvres*, that his timing was tactless, but he had too much pride, and too many people on his side, to hang his head. Nor was there the smallest risk that any bloody Jew would take violent action against him.

Scarfe's daring relied for its appeal on the timeless image of the vulturous, eternally culpable Jew. Modern 'satire' conceals an appetite for, above all, popularity.[62] In the usual places, Israelis are regularly said to target children. During the recent fighting in Gaza, four Palestinian children playing on the beach were said, by the English media, to have been killed by Israeli fire. It has now been conceded, very quietly, that they actually died when a Hamas rocket, which was being projected from nearby, misfired.

In March 2015, Trevor Phillips OBE – the former head of the Commission for Racial Equality, and still involved in institutional egalitarianism – appeared in person, on Channel 4, to break ranks, so he claimed, with the political rectitude about race that his office had paid him to

---

62 Rory Bremner, the outspoken, often witty mimic of domestic British politicians and pontificators, came clean recently when he confessed a reluctance to satirise people so incapable of taking a joke that they might come after you with a Kalashnikov.

peddle. In a long programme entitled *Things We Won't Say about Race That Are True*, he affected courage in shucking the inhibitions that required him to see no evil where it plainly existed in ethnic clusters. He chose to begin his retraction from being Mr Nice Guy in the New West End Synagogue. This grandiose, untypical place of Jewish worship is the long-standing bastion of London's most opulent Jews.

In the light of the anglicised, stained-glass windows, Phillips – playing the part of the deliverer of the low-down – announced that Jews in England were twice as rich as other people. Whether they earned their money or confected it by some alchemical means was left unclear. Phillips did not define a Jew or disclose from what agency he acquired his statistics; nor did he say why the above-average prosperity of Jews belonged in a programme that promised unpalatable revelations.

When the film cut to a river view of the Palace of Westminster, Phillips revealed that there were twenty-two Jewish Members of Parliament, which he held to be a 'disproportionate' number. The implication was that membership of the House should be regulated in accordance with statistics that distinguished between one category of

British subjects and another. His saleable decision to be frank allowed Phillips to assume that Jews constituted a sub-set of citizens that should have only an appropriate number of representatives in Parliament. He did not stipulate a figure, but the impression was given that some kind of justice, not particularly British, required that it be very small. He did not care to mention that Westminster's Jews figured in different parties, held differing, often opposing views, and were almost certain to vote in accordance with party allegiance rather in some cabalistic caucus.[63]

In effect, no doubt unintentionally, Phillips was under writing the fascist notion of 'the corporate state', in which various classes of citizen should be represented in accordance with their status and numbers. He seemed ignorant of, unless he was hostile to, the basic democratic notion that, whatever their social or other provenance, all citizens are, and should be, equally liable to advancement in whatever department of life they choose. Phillips did go

---

63 The coincidental similarity of 'Kabbalah' (a form of Jewish, especially Hasidic, mysticism) and 'cabal' (a term for conspirators, derived from the initials of a group of scheming politicians in the reign of Charles II) is too tasty not to figure in the mouths of agitated rhetoricians. In 2003, Tam Dalyell – then the father (oldest member) of the British House of Commons – declared that George W. Bush's America was run by a 'Jewish cabal' that manipulated the born-again Christian President and his neo-conservative Cabinet into overthrowing Saddam Hussein.

on to admit that there were gangs, among a certain strand of Pakistani immigrants, who 'groomed' and sold young white girls, and that most murders of black people were committed by other black people. Since he dealt almost entirely with delinquencies in other 'ethnic' groups, we were left with the clear impression that money and ambition had allowed Jews to rise to an unwarranted number of high places. For all anyone knows, or should care, the same thing may apply to people whose surnames begin with 'A' or some other disproportionately favoured initial.

*　　*　　*

19

THE POST-MODERN META-DEMOCRACY is one in which morality and *raison d'état* converge. It is becoming obligatory to allay the grievances of any large number of voters, even if, as is the case in France, they express them by beating up or killing other citizens who come in smaller categorical bundles. In England, too, any 'community' capable of becoming electorally significant is likely to win concessions, including limitations on freedom of speech (according to the new prudery, even to refer to someone as a Scot risks being termed 'racist').

Different communities tend to have leaders with at least one interest in common: the wish to increase their own political standing. This tends to encourage the creation of enclaves whose 'leaders' or 'clerics' can determine their conduct and, of course, deliver their votes. The erosion of the middle ground is confirmed by ceding territory to the reserves of specific 'ethnic' groups. Was it a joke when George Galloway spoke of a section of Bradford as being 'Israel-free', the better to cull Pakistani votes? The corruption in the town hall of Tower Hamlets, which was, in effect, a Muslim fiefdom, only recently became too blatant to slide under any convenient carpet.

Only those who speak up for Israel can, with impunity, be put down as a conspiratorial force behind whatever displeases men such as Oliver Miles, who was 'our man in Tripoli' under Colonel Gaddafi. Having left the diplomatic service and gone into the armaments business, Miles was outspoken in deploring the late Sir Martin Gilbert's place on Sir John Chilcot's board of inquiry into the 2003 Iraq

War. It was, he feared, impossible for a Zionist to be dispassionate. It would be safer if Jews were excluded from British public life. Miles's judgement was, of course, in no way inflected by his position as chairman of MEC International with wide business interests in Arab countries.

* * *

20

IN APRIL 1833, in the House of Commons, Thomas Babington Macaulay argued, with accurate passion, in favour of the emancipation of Britain's Jews. They comprised the last section of the male population still ineligible, on religious grounds, to become Members of the House. He confronted the supposed innate duplicity of Jews with civil logic:

> If there be any proposition universally true in politics, it is this: that foreign attachments are the fruit of domestic misrule. It has always been the trick of bigots to make their subjects miserable at home, and then to complain they

look to relief abroad, to divide society, and to wonder that it is not united ... If the Jews have not felt towards England like children, it is because she has treated them like a stepmother ... We treat them as slaves and wonder that they do not regard us as brethren. We drive them to mean occupations and then reproach them for not embracing honourable professions. We long forbade them to possess land; and we complain that they chiefly occupy themselves in trade. We shut them out from all the paths of ambition, and then we despise them for taking refuge in avarice.

In his peroration, Macaulay preferred not to broach the issue of religion and of the systematic debasement of 'the Jews' in Christian mythology. He relied, once again, on humane simplification:

If all the red-haired people in Europe had, during centuries, been outraged and oppressed, banished from this place, imprisoned in that, deprived of their money, deprived of their teeth, convicted of the most improbable crimes on the feeblest evidence, dragged at horses' tails, hanged, tortured, burned alive, if, when manners became milder, they had still been subject to debasing restrictions and exposed to vulgar insults, locked up in particular streets in some countries, pelted and ducked by the rabble in others, excluded everywhere from magistracies and honours, what would be the patriotism of gentlemen with red hair?

Macaulay's eloquence inspired the House of Commons to vote for the emancipation of Britain's Jews, but its punch did not carry as far as the House of Lords, where the bishops of the Church of England mounted a vocal crusade against the enrolment of the descendants of the Jerusalem mob, which the Gospels declared to have called unanimously for the death of Jesus Christ. The hostility of a broad band of principled sentiment persisted into the twentieth century. A hundred years after Macaulay sought to welcome British Jews into full citizenship, Adolf Hitler's rise to power in Germany lent muscle to a form of Judaeophobia more virulent than the most vindictive inquisitor had ever dared to promote. When Hitler's crooked crusade led to a flood of refugees seeking haven elsewhere, the General Synod of the Church of England set its face against their admission. Only the then Archbishop of York opposed an embargo.

T. S. Eliot, a Yankee immigrant eager to proclaim himself an Anglo-Catholic royalist, lent fastidious authority to the current idea that it would be unwise, if not subversive, to suffer too many 'free-thinking Jews' to have access to what he outlined as an ideal Christian society. His affectations of perfect pitch led him to say of Macaulay that he was the outstanding instance of a prose stylist corrupted by journalism. The implication was that only a crowd-pleasing opportunist would propose a policy of such promiscuous generosity. There is petty comedy in observing that, among the most virulent literary anti-Semites in pre-war British society, Hilaire Belloc, Ezra Pound and the clerically cut Mr Eliot were all *arrivistes*. William Joyce, a one-time lieutenant of Oswald Mosley in the British Union of Fascists, was an Irish immigrant whose nationality rendered him, in some legal eyes, unqualified to be a traitor to Great Britain,[64] despite his loud place in pre-war insular politics.

Another twenty-five years had had to pass after Macaulay's 1833 speech before the Upper House agreed to allow Jews to be eligible for election. Ten years later, in 1868,

---

64 In 1946, he was hanged all the same. During the war, his curiously pronounced, pro-Nazi broadcasts from Berlin earned him the title 'Lord Haw-Haw'.

Benjamin Disraeli became Queen Victoria's Prime Minister. Disraeli had been baptised into the Church of England in 1816, at the age of twelve, by his father (Byron's friend and favourite author, Isaac D'Israeli), who had had an acrimonious falling-out with the council of the City of London's oldest synagogue, Bevis Marks. More personal than doctrinal, the dispute issued from Isaac's decision not to suffer his son's horizons to be limited by parochial allegiance.

❊   ❊   ❊

21

ALTHOUGH BAPTISED AS a Christian, Disraeli was regularly vilified, not least by his high-minded Liberal opponent William Gladstone, as the very type of the shifty, opportunistic Jew. Disraeli's response was stylish: rather than apologise for his roots, he held them up for admiration. He even dared to say that his ancestors were princes in Palestine, while the forebears even of his patron and predecessor (the noble Earl of Derby) were prancing around in woad. Disraeli combined insolence with wit to such good effect that the cry 'Dizzy's up!' was enough to bring Members of Parliament crowding back into the chamber. As Macaulay wrote about Horatius in his *Lays of Ancient Rome*, 'e'en the ranks of Tuscany could scarce forbear to cheer'. Disraeli entertained where Gladstone moralised. His flamboyant eloquence and macaronic dress flaunted what others might have preferred to conceal. By his mastery of the English language, he rendered himself legendary. He remains, with Winston Churchill, one of the few British prime ministers to be identified, even today, by an affectionate diminutive.

British Jews have lived, with a certain complacency, under the aegis of Queen Victoria's favourite Prime Minister. As Disraeli forecast, many of the supposedly disloyal aliens, once enfranchised, proved eager to be conservative pillars of the society that had sought to exclude them. Disraeli's own progress along the primrose path was by no means universally applauded. It amused him to pander to his wizard image in the swaggering self-portraits he found time to publish in his novels. While it piqued him to give the impression of being armed with quasi-supernatural powers, his conceits lent credence to the fear that there was, as Ann Widdecombe would come to say about the then leader of her own political party Michael Howard, 'something of the night' about him. Mr Howard happened to be a liberal Jew, as well as a QC, with no known nocturnal peculiarities.

Anthony Trollope pandered to his readers by depicting 'Dizzy' as the cosmopolitan, financial trickster Augustus Melmotte. In fact, Disraeli did use his connections with the Rothschilds to supply the instant funds that procured a 50 per cent share of the Suez Canal Company for Great Britain. His patriotic purpose was to secure a share of control over the means of easier access to the Indian Empire than the long way around the Cape of Good Hope. The tradition of Christian and post-Christian contempt for Jews persisted in English literature, high and low, for more than 500 years.

By portraying Jews as scheming money-grubbers, interwar novelists, from John Buchan to Graham Greene and J. B. Priestley, chose to flatter their readers' prejudices rather than to mount any solemn accusation. When Rudyard Kipling accused D. H. Lawrence of being 'pro-Yid' (for favouring a Jewish presence in the Middle East), he was putting on Foreign Office airs. There was no Jewish

'Gunga Din'. British imperialism sustained its vanity not least because its lordly directors saw nothing improper in acquiring land, although its commercial exploitation was beneath them. The landlessness of 'the Jews' and their identification with trade and finance proved their inferiority.

Jews were, in Kipling's terms, European untouchables. Inescapably defined as civilians, they could always be accused of cowardice. Who, including the poet himself, ever mentioned that Siegfried Sassoon, for heroic instance, was of Jewish descent? Lawrence, although often accused of fascistic tendencies, spoke of the Jewish genius for 'disinterested speculation'. If that phrase carries a tincture of irony, Lawrence's admiration for the Jewish General Monash, who commanded the Australian Army in the Great War, is manifest in a leading character in the novel *Kangaroo* (1923).

Contempt for Jews was encouraged by the success of fascism and, even in Britain and America, continued throughout the war, aided by the revelations associated with newsreels of Belsen concentration camp, outside Munich. The subsequent 'liberation' of Auschwitz and other death factories in the East proved that Belsen was by no means the worst of the camps, since it was not expressly designed for the murder and incineration of Jews. Hence, by an ironic turn, Belsen came to be used by Holocaust deniers as 'proof' that the story of six million murdered Jews was a fabrication designed to extract sympathy and – Jews being Jews – cash from 'innocent' Germans and others.

We are never quite out of earshot of the loud whisper that if Israel did not exist, all would become nice and orderly again. This claim carries a rider that the wish to destroy 'the Zionists' has nothing whatsoever in common with the old-fashioned anti-Semitism. The deposit is that, after this cathartic purge, civilised people – good Jews included – will be left to enjoy the contraction and laming of Israel, preliminary to the warranted destruction of the arrogant 'Zionist entity'. Once that small enclave – abhorrent alike to Muslims everywhere and to the double rump of the old left and the old right – has been effaced, any Jews who survive will be suffered to return to a subservient place in post-Christian society and become, as before, dependent on disdainful indifference on the part of their hosts. In Jungian terms, some part of the European group mind looks forward backwards to a time when there was no need to feel guilty about what happened to the Jews. Nostalgia takes many forms.

❖   ❖   ❖

22

THERE IS AN old story about Adolf Hitler, in post-war hiding, telling someone that, 'next time', he will finish off the Jews and also two ballet dancers. 'Why two ballet dancers?' says the other man. 'See what I mean?' says Adolf. 'Who cares what happens to Jews?'

This chestnut's enduring relevance lies in the fact that, for all the generous space ceded to him, Professor Tombs found no room in his *ex cathedra* remarks about the *Charlie Hebdo* shooting to even mention the murders in the kosher supermarket of four people who had satirised no one. Their only provocative characteristic was that they were likely to be Jews. Were they Zionists? Who really cares? The media echoes that old cry of Innocent III to kill them all, without the saving grace of '*novit enim Dominus qui sunt ejus*'.

Cultural pundits, echoing its malevolent neighbours, maintain that the Israeli state has no right to exist. Such a charge has not been levelled against any other of the 193 states of the United Nations. Many of them are post-colonial fabrications with boundaries arbitrarily allotted by their quondam European conquerors. Israel's alleged iniquity is held to disqualify it from the family of nations in which the Democratic Republic of the Congo has an unquestioned place, although several million of its people have been killed by their fellow citizens. Was there a sustained cry of outrage in the western press when Hafez al-Assad, the tyrant of Syria from 1971 to 2000, conducted a full-scale military campaign in 1982 against the city of Hama, in which 30,000 'rebel' Syrians are said to have been killed? How many of them were children? While Assad's prisoners (suspected opponents) were tortured and executed without trial, his admirers – anti-Israel in particular – continued to regard him as a 'strong man' and to demand that the Golan Heights, from which Assad's artillery used to threaten large tracts of Israel's heartland, be returned to Syrian control. What affected to be a call to honour international law was designed to put Israel in mortal danger.

In all the wars between Israel and her neighbours, unbiased estimates hold that fewer than 70,000 people have died. Adolf Eichmann is the only killer to have been executed (in 1962) since the foundation of the state in 1948.

It is, however, true that Israel conducted an undercover vendetta against those responsible for killing her unarmed athletes at the 1972 Munich Olympic Games. Arabs, meanwhile, have been murderously divided among themselves. They find unity in only one dogmatic credo, endorsed by sighing western pundits – that the destruction of Israel will restore peace and harmony to the world. The Nazi recipe – that getting rid of the Jews, in whatever form, will purge the world of evil – has been served up again.

Hitler and his gang claimed that the Zionist leader Chaim Weizmann's declaration at the outbreak of the Second World War that he hoped for an Allied victory proved that 'the Jews' had declared war on Germany, and so struck the first blow in the events that led to the Holocaust. It is tempting to regard this as cynical humbug, but the sorry truth may well be that they believed it. After the war, Ernst Nolte, a respectable German historian, found it somewhat understandable that, viewing the Jews (rightly or wrongly) as an internal enemy, Hitler had to authorise a pre-emptive strike against them before they made any trouble. Nolte might have mentioned that it required taking a very long view to kill more than a million children. He did observe, quite truly, that the Russians had anticipated the Germans in creating a system of concentration camps for slave labourers. Other apologists for fascism have pointed out that the expression 'concentration camp' dates from the Boer War in South Africa, when the British forced Dutch settlers off disputed territory and into barbed-wire enclosures. This has not disposed any Wilson or Paulin to equate them with Nazis.

Israel is forever being accused of ethnic cleansing and of being the sole reason why Palestinian 'refugees' are still herded (what else?) into 'camps'. One of the reasons why these encampments continue to exist, and grow more crowded, is that almost no neighbouring power has shown willingness to welcome their Arab brethren, or even to give many of them exit visas to move to other destinations. Although a small, poor, aid-dependent country, Jordan has done more than any oil-rich state to harbour Arab refugees, not least large numbers from Iraq and Syria. This has rarely earned audible gratitude.[65]

---

65 The Palestinian terrorist movement labelled 'Black September' was so named after a war between Jordanian (mainly Bedouin) forces and Yasser Arafat's Al-Fatah organisation, which was threatening to take control of its host country. Al-Fatah was expelled, mainly into Lebanon, where it also attempted, with some success, to establish a state within a state, until most of its militants were driven out by Israel in the 1982 Lebanon War. Desperate people do desperate things; but their leaders do not always accumulate enormous personal fortunes, as Arafat did.

No Jew is allowed to set foot in the Saudi Kingdom, a monarchy established after the Great War by the British as part of the 'loot' (Franco-British slang for the remnants of the Ottoman Empire). Like the expulsion and expropriation of almost a million Jews once resident in Arab countries, this embargo has not excited any sarcastic quibble from conscientious Europeans. Caryl Churchill, for instance, prefers to depict Israeli children being indoctrinated with a murderous hatred of all Arabs. Her applauded play on this theme was a mirror reversal of a routine element in the curriculum of Islamic 'faith' schools.[66] The Quran certifies that killing Jews can be a virtuous activity. Why else have we seen, sprayed on bus stops in Birmingham, the injunction to 'Kill Jews'?[67] It's in the Book.

---

66 In *Seven Jewish Children*, she quotes what is meant to be a typical Jew: 'Tell her I look at one of their children covered in blood and what do I feel? ... Tell her I wouldn't care if we wiped them out ... Tell her I don't care if the world hates us, tell us we're better haters, tell her we're chosen people.' This, like so much anti-Semitism, is marked neither by accuracy nor by wit. One of the few durable Jew-conscious remarks of any wit is that made by David Lloyd George, who said of his fellow Liberal, Herbert Samuel (a man distinguished, as Lloyd George never was, by his sense of honour and impartiality) that "when they circumcised him, they threw away the wrong bit".

67 The traditional Jewish notion that it was sinful to kill played at least some part in what Hannah Arendt and others have called the 'sheep-like docility' of European Jews when they were abandoned to their fate. The film *Perlasca*, starring Luca Zingaretti (television's Inspector Montalbano), based on the true story of an Italian (fascist) Schindler, has a telling moment when a young Jew renounces non-violence and its consequent fatalism.

Today's anti-Semitism is 'new' only because the modern advocate of Jew-killing is likely to be scrupulous in denying that he is an anti-Semite. An elaborate distinction has been drawn between anti-Zionism – an honourable contagion – and the hatred of Jews in general. In accordance with that principle, Günter Grass, the author of the anti-Nazi novel *The Tin Drum*, announced not long ago before his death (15 April 2015) that Israel was the greatest, if not the only, threat to world peace. The voice of Germany's post-war conscience belonged to the same man who had long concealed the fact that, in 1944, he was recruited, willingly, into the Waffen SS. It seems that, by luck rather than through the exercise of any exceptional moral scruple, he took no part in the massacres of unarmed civilians, especially Jews, which formed a regular part of the duties of SS men. Can we be sure that the good soldier Grass would have refused an order to kill unarmed people who had committed no crime except to belong to a damnable category? He was never put to that test, or so we are expected to believe. The question remains: how did it come about that so many of his countrymen, and their alien recruits, saw nothing wrong in mass murder?

* * *

23

IN *ON THE EVE* (2012), a study of European Jewry on the eve of the war, Bernard Wasserstein begins by parodying Marxist apocalyptics:

> A spectre haunted Europe in the 1930s – the spectre of the Jew. Simultaneously feared and despised as a Christ-killer, a devil with horns, subversive revolutionary and capitalist exploiter, obdurate upholder of an outmoded religion and devious exponent of cultural modernism, the Jew was widely regarded as an alien presence ... Transmogrified from fellow citizen into bogey, a subhuman, at best an inconvenience, eventually almost everywhere a hunted beast ... true not just in those areas of Europe directly ruled by the Nazis, but over the greater part of the continent.

In *l'entre-deux-guerres*, the Nazis, their imitators and admirers, albeit offstage, altered the consciousness and constricted the options of Jews almost everywhere. At the same time, in Wasserstein's words, 'the cultural glue [including the Yiddish and Judaeo-Espagnol languages] that had long bound the Jews together was losing its cohesive power'. In the darkest hour of their common peril, European Jews became easy victims of what Sartre later called 'serialisation': many were gulled by the belief that, in the cradle of civilisation, nicely spoken citizens, not least those with decorations for gallantry in the First World War, would remain exempt from persecution. Many assimilated German Jews presumed that they could, as their ancestors had, live with the laws that humiliated them and the culture they loved. Their own press advised them to wear the Yellow Star with pride. Despite the omens so accurately read by the outspoken novelist and journalist Joseph Roth (1894–1939), few could believe that the Third Reich was governed by a band of predatory and murderous fanatics.

In 1938, the sociologist Norbert Elias begged his visiting parents to stay in England, where he had found refuge, but his father insisted on returning to Breslau: 'I have never done anything wrong. What can they do to me?' Consciously or not, Elias senior was paraphrasing the opening words of Kafka's *The Trial* (published in 1925): 'Someone must have been telling lies about Josef K. because one day he was arrested, *although he had done nothing wrong.*' Elias's father could not credit that he, like all Jews in Christian and Nazi mythology, *was* something wrong.

The title *On the Eve* was borrowed from the novel of Ivan Turgenev, who claimed that 'art is one **of the four** things that unite men'. It did not occur to the arch-liberal that anti-Semitism was another. His *frère ennemi* Dostoyevsky might have told him so. Dostoyevsky had been sentenced to death and subjected to a mock-execution for plotting against the Tsar. Although Jews had nothing to do with the case, he emerged from it with a mixture of pan-Slavist and Orthodox Christian convictions; they shared belief in an 'ideal' enemy – the Jews (Tolstoy was a rare, overt philo-Semite). What specific Jews did/did not do is never relevant to what the 'logic' of anti-Semitism promised they wanted or intended to do, unless they were killed first.

Jonathan Sacks has claimed that the great and distinctive quality of Jews is their 'solidarity'. It is a pious sentiment, but a myopic observation. Chief Rabbi from 1991 to 2013 of Great Britain's ultra-orthodox community, Sacks is a pleasant, erudite and broad-minded man in private life. However, his notion of solidarity did not permit him to attend the funeral of the 'reform' Rabbi Hugo Gryn, a

Holocaust survivor of rare courage, whose doctrinal differences rendered him anathema to Sacks's faction. Under pressure from his committee, Sacks had to appear somewhat ashamed to even have given his condolences in person to Gryn's family.

Antagonisms of more or less refined kinds have often set Jew against Jew, politically, socially and intellectually, seldom more often than in the 1930s. Even among Polish Jewry, which was 'least affected by assimilation ... the proudest of Jewish communities', Bundists (Jewish socialist trades unionists), Zionists, the bourgeoisie and introspective traditionalists never trusted each other to mount a common defence against an increasingly reactionary government. When it comes to the fractiousness of the orthodox rabbinate, Bernard Wasserstein supplies tragi-comic chapter and verse:

> Some [Hasidim] frowned on intermarriage with the followers of other ... *rebbes*, feuded bitterly with them, even engaged in physical violence, and, worst of all, impugned the *kashrut* of a rival *rebbe*'s *tish* [table]. When the third Belzer *rebbe* ... fled from Galicia to Munkács in 1920, the Munkácser *rebbe* refused to countenance the presence of

a rival on his turf. 'There is no room for the two of us in this one place!' [The incumbent] mobilised influence on the government to secure the *arriviste*'s expulsion from Czechoslovakia.

The fate of so many of the *Ostjuden* and of the *shtetl* (village) societies that Sholem Aleichem's stories celebrated has encouraged the folkloric retrospection to be seen in Chagall's colourful elegies, and tunefully sugared in *Fiddler on the Roof*. In dull truth, the life of Jews in the East was often nasty, brutish and shortened by, for notorious instance, the Chmelnicki Cossacks. Sholem's beloved *Ostjuden* might have been sly and superstitious, but they were less drunk or bestial than the surrounding Russians and Ukrainians. In *Fathers and Sons*, Turgenev recalls the saying: 'The Russian peasant will get the better of God himself.' Violence and double-dealing were commonplace. Even Ivan Turgenev's aristocratic mother often beat him brutally, for no reason at all except to assert herself. Anti-Semitism was a pious aspect of the socially organised sadism of the whole Tsarist Empire.

Sholem Aleichem himself witnessed a *pogrom* in Kiev in 1905 so frightful that he quit Russia forever. When the inhabitants, who, in reality, were bleak and impoverished, spilled westwards, their *Yiddishkeit* (low-class Jewishness) proved alarmingly alien to assimilated co-religionists, such as Robert de Rothschild, who said, in 1935: 'If they are not happy here [in France], let them leave. They are guests whom we have warmly received but they should not go about rocking the boat.' The condescensions of the more-or-less assimilated Jewish bourgeoisie led Joseph Roth to embrace the authenticity of the pedlars, tinkers and smugglers of his native Galicia as against the Viennese softness of, in particular, his benefactor Stefan Zweig. *Yiddishkeit* has sentimentalised life in the Old Country, but who would wish to return to it? One of its greatest literary celebrants, Sholem Asch, ended up living in a villa on the French Riviera. During the Russian Revolution, the Jewish short-story writer Isaac Babel rode with the revolutionary Cossacks, whose forerunners mounted savage *pogroms* under the legendary Bogdan Chmelnicki. They became the subject of the terse and covertly ironic stories in *Red Cavalry*. During the Terror, he was forced, as he put it, to make silence into a new art form. This did not save him from being murdered, in 1940, by Stalin's NKVD for being a 'Trotskyist' (transparent code for Jew).

Sentimentalists are likely to ignore the humiliation of Jewish women in the Old Country. They were deemed better if they remained uninformed. Few males questioned what Rabbi Eliezer had said in the first century CE: 'He who teaches his daughter Torah is teaching her promiscuity.' As in the Essene enclaves in Flavius Josephus's time, female prattle was not to be taken seriously. 'Better a son who is a bath-house attendant', said Eliezer, 'than a daughter married to a rabbi.' Orthodox brides had to have their heads shaved, an allegedly antique ritual that originated only in the late eighteenth century. Mirel Hurvitz, the heroine of David Bergelson's 1913 novel *The End of Everything*, stood for her own and her author's appetite for something beyond the atavistic world in which even the 'enlightened' young (especially females) were clamped. Freud's now derided notion of 'penis envy' makes more sense as a symptom of *social* rather than of sexual deprivation. To be born a man was indeed enviable when females were of negligible account. 'Weep, bride, weep!' was the advice of the mendicant entertainers known, in Yiddish, as *Badkhn*.

Meanwhile, Wasserstein tells us, 'in much of ... Europe, [women] were in the vanguard of the modernisation and acculturation of Jewish society'. He has harsh words, however, for the French *philosophe* Simone Weil (1909–43). Susan Sontag said that Weil lived 'a life absurd in its exaggerations and degree of self-mutilation'. Might it be that it took one to spot one? Weil tried desperately to detach herself from her Semitic shadow (as a teacher, she wanted to substitute Plato for the Old Testament). This revulsion from Judaism, which took her only as far as the threshold of the Church, had a good deal in common with the less spiritual *démarche* that impelled Irène Némirovsky into what she hoped would be the haven of Catholicism.

Although baptised, Némirovsky was dumped in 1940 by all but one or two of her non-Jewish friends. She sought refuge in *la France profonde*, where her faith in Gentiles was not confirmed: 'Everyone lives in his own house, on his own land, distrusts his neighbours, harvests his wheat, counts his money and doesn't give a thought to the rest of the world.' As a smart pre-war Parisian novelist, Némirovsky had been scathing about Jews, not least her own father, whom she satirised in the bestselling *David Golder* (1929). In hiding, she realised the truth about many things, but, before she could tell it in full, she was betrayed and

deported. Her children survived with the incomplete man-
uscript, which was published in 2006 as *Suite française*.

* * *

24

I N *THE CHATHAM HOUSE VERSION* (1970), the one-time
Iraqi Jew Elie Kedourie considered the largely Brit-
ish-inspired break-up of the Ottoman Empire – the most
lamentable political consequence of the peace concluded
at Versailles in 1919. Woodrow Wilson's doctrine of 'the
self-determination of peoples' was a particular, if unin-
tended, disaster for Europe's Jews. The disintegration of
the baggy monster that had been the Austro-Hungarian
Empire led to the petty nationalisms of the Balkan states,
whose leaders had in common the boast that they were
not Jews. The social slights that Arthur Koestler endured
with clinical disdain in old Vienna turned septic in the
truncated republic that was left behind. Woodrow Wilson's good intentions led to what became, in the words
of David S. Wyman, the abandonment of the Jews. If

they could not live in Europe, where were they to go if not to hell?

Zionism, with its socialist and secular overtones, was a little-regarded 'solution' for most Jews until soon before the outbreak of war in 1939. In eastern Europe, the more attractive alternative to orthodoxy was communism. In the early days, many Jews had good, local reason to embrace Lincoln Steffens's view that the Soviet Union represented 'the future that works'. In 1920, all religious activity, including that of the Orthodox Church, was being dismantled in the USSR. At last, it seemed, Jews were to be no different from anyone else. In 1921, a show trial of a *yeshiva* (Talmudic academy) was literally staged, in Yiddish, in the local theatre in Vitebsk. Evidence of the merits of one particular teacher was met with: 'You can't whiten a slop bucket with a spoonful of sour cream.' The local rabbi, Shmaryahu Leib Medalia, responded: 'The Torah has lived and shall live.' But the verdict was that all the local children should be despatched to Yiddish secular schools; victory was celebrated over 'Jewish clericalism, Zionism and nationalism'.

Their literate and professional skills made many of the USSR's three million Jews willing servants of the *apparat.* While a large number were deemed *lishentsy* (non-proletarians deserving of expropriation), even they could, in theory, recover their civil rights after five years of 'productive labour'. At least until the mid-1940s, Stalin was happy to make use of his Jews' commitment and intelligence. In 1928, as an alternative to Zionism, a remote border area of Birobidzhan, adjacent to Manchuria, was designated the 'Autonomous Jewish Region'. Its 36,000 square kilometres made it slightly larger than mandatory Palestine. In the 1930s, its Jewish population — mostly poor immigrants from other parts of the USSR – was more than 30,000, although hunger and disease made it a parody of Zion.

In 1937, accusations of Trotskyism led to the arrest of the local party chief Matvei Khavkin, who, 'most incriminating of all', was reported to have greeted a comrade with '*Gut Shabbes*'. His wife was accused of having tried to poison the visiting (originally Jewish) central committee member Lazar Kaganovich with homemade *gefilte* fish. In 1938, the settlement was placed under Secret Police control. Of the 319 delegates sent to the Second Congress of Soviets of Biro in 1936, 227 had been arrested by the end of 1938; 116 of them were shot. The region's only remaining Jewish policeman was reported in 1937 to have been eaten by a Siberian tiger.

In western Europe, Jews took, or hoped to take, various ways out of social and intellectual peculiarity. The white coat of the scientists was an emancipation from Shylock's Jewish gabardine. 'Science' was a fraternity in which, as in Pauline Christianity, there was neither Jew nor Gentile. 'The Truth' – unlike the journalistic style that Karl Kraus called *mauscheln* – had no telltale Jewish accent.

Early in the twentieth century, the 'Jewish question' posed itself differently to different people, and especially to intellectuals – for instance, Otto Weininger, who committed suicide in 1903 at the age of twenty-three, after writing one memorable book.[68] In *Geschlecht und Charakter* (*Sex and Character*), he attributed virility only to Aryans. Jews were located in an effeminate annex. Weininger's distinctions, like Freud's, were an amalgam of literary insights and metaphysical 'science'. Without denying his Jewish origin, Weininger crossed the line, if only with one foot. His suicide secured his Tiresian reputation.

Graced with the aura of a last testament, his text had

---

68 Carlo Michelstaedter, a Triestine Jewish prodigy who wrote just one brilliant book, *Persuasion and Rhetoric*, committed suicide in 1910 at the same age as Weininger.

great appeal for anti-Semites. Since it came, on a Nazi reading, as a confession from the other side, Weininger has been read as giving comfort to the enemy. Because Weininger's 'mishmash' was 'discussed by Hitler' is insufficient reason to dismiss him, Béla Szabados notes, in *Wittgenstein Reads Weininger* (2004), that Weininger was respected, if only for his 'valuable errors', by Ludwig Wittgenstein.[69]

In the 1920s and 1930s, the Vienna Circle of 'logical positivists' attacked the dominant religion by indirection. Its overt animus was against 'metaphysics' – the system-building 'revelations' of other philosophers. Logic, not rhetoric, articulated the syntax of logical positivism; its aggressive neutrality sharpened the guillotine that was meant to sever metaphysicians from respectable academic company. Its English apostle, the precocious A. J. Ayer, denied that the logical positivists were ever motivated by a desire to assimilate to a universal 'religion' of science or for its company to dress itself in the uniformity of men who, with no distinction between Jew and Gentile, worked

---

69 Béla Szabados says that Wittgenstein was indignant to discover that *Sex and Character* was lodged in a part of the Cambridge University Library inaccessible to undergraduates. He was, however, unsurprised when G. E. Moore failed to admire the book, but maintained that it deserved to be taken seriously, even if it was wise to put a '~' (the logical symbol for negation) in front of Weininger's whole thesis. There were, Wittgenstein implied, interesting ways of being wrong.

in the world's supreme laboratory. The Vienna Circle's cult of science, like Freud's, can be read, from outside, as another attempted great escape from specificity into a godless monotheism to which Yahweh, like the Saviour, was irrelevant. Whatever he considered his motives to be,[70] Ayer's attitude resembles Wittgenstein's ambivalent allegiance to the Vienna Circle, which he attended and then repudiated.

One of the most admired and most anguished intellectuals of *l'entre-deux-guerres*, Walter Benjamin, echoed his ideas: 'For all their education and refinement, for all their prominence in the cultural sphere, German Jews are less than well-formed human beings. They are debilitated hermaphrodites.'

To overcome their half-and-halfness, Benjamin argued for an 'area in which the Jewish mind can be isolated and show itself in its true nature'. He conceded that 'highly valuable strengths in Judaism are being lost through assimilation', but could not work out how, 'from here, one

---

70 The positivists' relegation of 'morals' to matters of personal opinion was, by coincidence, much to the hedonistic taste of both Ayer and his *maître à penser* Bertrand Russell. The commandments of revealed religion were relegated to mere fetishes. Freud put his patients on the couch; modern philosophers have shown an aptitude for joining their pupils there.

arrives at Zionism'. Benjamin considered Palestine the right answer only for persecuted *Ostjuden*. For intellectuals, he proposed a sublime *Kulturreich*, immune to the savage reality from which – slumped in Portbou in 1940 – he proved unable to escape. His friend Gershom Scholem, who had emigrated to Palestine years earlier, had tried in vain to persuade Benjamin to abandon his Marxist illusions and accept that Jews could not rely on the notion of a homogeneous European civilisation.

*   *   *

25

THE HISTORY OF the Holocaust has a history of its own. Despite the ostentatious exercise of wringing their hands at the Évian Conference in 1938, western democracies offered virtually no practical aid to the increasingly desperate victims of fascism. By 1939, Wasserstein tells us: 'More and more Jews were ... reduced to wandering refugees ... more were held in camps outside the Third Reich than within it.' In public, the British government made noble noises; but, as the net tightened, the Foreign Office furtively urged Balkan countries to make it as difficult as possible for Jews to escape to Palestine. The British have vaunted themselves on their grace in allowing the *Kindertransport* (a private initiative) to bring some 10,000 German Jewish children to England, but they were obdurate that the children's parents should stay where they were. When it was proposed that 20,000 Jewish children be allowed into the US, socially and financially influential WASPs (White Anglo-Saxon Protestants) aborted the programme, saying that the young might be beautiful in their innocence, but were bound to grow up to be ugly and hook-nosed.

Between 1945 and 1960, only a few books – one of the first was Lord Russell of Liverpool's *The Scourge of the Swastika* – dealt, superficially or in piecemeal fashion, with the murder of between five and six million Jews by the Nazis and their confederates. In the 1950s, the Cold War led the western world to abate their zeal (never great in the case of the British) for the pursuit of 'war criminals'. This comfortable, because baggy, usage suggests that the culpability of killing and robbing millions of defenceless civilians should be seen only in the context of the surrounding war. In fact, while the war granted a screen for uninhibited butchery, greed and sadism, the crimes themselves were of no rare, still less excusable order.

Anna Bikont's *Le Crime et le silence* (2011) is an unblinking account of a specific and particularly horrible massacre, by their Polish neighbours, of the 16,000 Jewish inhabitants of the village of Jedwabne in July 1941.[71] The Germans authorised the *pogrom* but, contrary to contemporary Polish claims, had no part in the process of, for instance, throwing babies into the flames of a burning building. It has, of course, been said that the Jewish villagers were pro-Soviet traitors and brought the trouble on themselves. The same was said of earlier generations, some of whom acted as rent- and tax-collectors on behalf of Polish landlords and noblemen. This earned them murderous treatment never visited on their employers. Their apologists remain in the habit of suggesting that, when it comes to the Jews, Poles were more sinned against than sinning. After the war, Poles and Russians (especially Ukrainians)

---

71 See also Jan T. Gross's *Neighbors: the Destruction of the Jewish Community in Jedwabne, Poland* (2001). Gross has also written at length about Polish anti-Semitism during and after the war.

avoided specifying that Jews were a particular target for hatred by amalgamating all the victims of fascism under a convenient common heading.

In 1961, two events imposed the *Shoah* on the public consciousness: the trial of Adolf Eichmann in Jerusalem; and the publication of Raul Hilberg's *The Destruction of the European Jews*. Both were denounced by Hannah Arendt – a Jewish refugee who had established herself as a prominent New York intellectual. A Zionist in her German youth, Arendt doubted the propriety of Eichmann's trial taking place in Jerusalem, despite the fact that there was small likelihood any other power would have staged it or even have arrested the defendant. In his biography of Eichmann, David Cesarani establishes that the Israelis themselves were in no hurry to bring him to justice. At the trial, the theatricality of the ambience and the histrionics of the prosecuting counsel were obnoxious to Arendt; so was the unashamed presence in Jerusalem of 'oily Jews' – a routine anti-Semitic term[72] by which she distanced herself from surviving members of the more than three million Yiddish-speakers who had, before 1939, lived in eastern

---

72 For an anti-Semitic precedent echo, see section 2, above.

Europe, mostly in Poland and the Ukraine. Arendt's distaste was of a piece with the long-standing German Jewish
tradition of aversion from *Ostjuden*.

Arendt's account of the Eichmann trial, commis-
sioned by the *New Yorker*, excited indignation among
other Jews, notably Walter Benjamin's friend Gershom
Scholem. The usually emollient Isaiah Berlin never for-
gave her for scorning people such as his mild Latvian
relatives because they failed to take up arms or enrol
allies from among the Gentiles (who, especially in the
Baltic states, took brutal pleasure in robbing and murdering them) when the Nazis gave them licence. Berlin
was the epitome of the assimilated Jewish intellectual –
the first Jew to be made a fellow of All Souls College,
Oxford. Winston Churchill took great pleasure in reading Berlin's despatches from wartime Washington DC.
Berlin came to epitomise the liberal Jewish attitude both
to philosophy and to the state of Israel, which he sup-
ported with critical partiality.

Arendt advised the Princeton University Press against
publishing *The Destruction of the European Jews* because
it was 'not sufficiently important'. She deplored it, in a
letter to Karl Jaspers, 'because [Hilberg] is pretty stupid

and crazy. He babbles now about a "death wish" of the Jews. His book is really excellent, but only because it is a simple report. A more general, introductory chapter is beneath a singed pig.' If Arendt did not care to speculate on the psychology of the victims, she did imply that the Jews somehow acquiesced in their fate. In this she conformed, however unwittingly, to the long tradition that has always found reasons for the Jews themselves to be responsible for their misfortunes.

* * *

26

IN MAY 1968, French left-wing students and *intellos* staged a march against General de Gaulle's regime – and, especially, against the deportation of student leader Danny 'the Red' Cohn-Bendit – under the banner: '*Nous sommes tous des Juifs allemands.*' That particular parade primed Alain Finkielkraut to break step: the marchers were not German Jews and they were just showing off. Today's students, not least in Great Britain, are disposed to chant:

'We are all Palestinians.' With the collapse of the Soviet model and the copious dilutions of democratic socialism, 'anti-Zionism' is the only 'revolutionary' doctrine that still has practical charm. It licenses students and their mentors in the academic world to intimidate Jewish students and brand Israel for defending its citizens. How many even know that Israel is the one state in the Middle East whose Christian population has never been physically in danger and is, in fact, growing quickly? The regular accusation that Israel practises apartheid ignores the fact that 20 per cent of its citizens are Arabs, and that its Jewish population is remarkably heterogeneous in appearance, habits and language. Grievances and conflicts are not uncommon, but Israeli democracy allows dissent, sometimes virulent, without murderous antagonism. How many thousands of Palestinians and other Arabs – Christian, Muslim and what all else – have been murdered by their 'brothers' in Syria, Iraq and elsewhere without evoking high-minded anathemas from *bien-pensant* circles?

The sole licensed target for unguarded malice in the world's media is the state of Israel. This need for a common target is relevant, to some degree, to what is going on in the political confusions of disunited Europe. There is an unstated nostalgia for a 'single cause', which might account for what is dislocating and depressing the Old Continent. The need for a wicked scapegoat, of small actual power and with little murderous purpose, accompanies the long guilt about the Holocaust and coalesces in the notion, in amiable British terms, that the Jews, like Israel, are more trouble than they are worth; hence, simultaneously, warrant preserving as an awful warning. The modern media supply the pillory.

Whatever the dread of the West with regard to Islam, it is shadowed by something one could typify, nicely, as resentment of 'the Jews'. They have persisted despite the 'truth' of Christianity, and, in the present state of that faith, can be said, perhaps, to have been right. What if there is no salvation and the notion of love superseding the law always was a piety too far? Man cannot function by emotions and fine feelings; the state of law must come first. But impatient, self-confident young men rarely think so. Shame about the Holocaust is very nice; not so nice is the repressed wish that the extermination of the Jews had been *justified*, in which case no one would have had to feel guilty. The conduct of the state of Israel has been welcomed, and its 'racism' exaggerated, because it furnishes a retroactive sentiment that 'we' (Europeans) need not feel bad about Auschwitz, nor about the lack of zeal with which Nazi murderers and their confederates were pursued by those who, with the onset of the Cold War in 1945, had better things to do, not least recruiting ex-Nazis to operate against the USSR.[73]

The reupholstered 'blood libel' went down big with London audiences and trendy critics of Caryl Churchill's curt insight into the murderous indoctrination of Jewish school kids.[74] She has yet to write a play about the Islamic schools where Jew hatred is an official part of the curriculum, and Jew murder recommended to graduates. Have a satirical go at some people and they really may come and kill you. The new anti-Semitism disposes first of all of anti-Semitism, and then, if that's what the people want, of the people who have always caused it.

---

73 See, for instance, Tom Bower's *Blind Eye to Murder* (1981) and *Justice Delayed* (1992) by David Cesarani. The Russians, of course, also recruited ex-Nazis, to confront the West. Those who were less solicited went to work for the Arabs or in South America. Jews were not much wanted anywhere, not least in England where, as Cesarani shows, a regiment of SS men was a more delectable import.

74 In *Seven Jewish Children*, Ms Churchill quotes what is supposed to be said by a typical Jew: "Tell her I look at one of their children covered in blood and what do I feel?... Tell her I wouldn't care if we wiped them out.... Tell her I don't care if the world hates us, tell us we're better haters, tell her we're chosen people." It is a small consolation to observe the witless terms with which tendentious malice is likely to be phrased.

❖ ❖ ❖

27

IN COMPOSING THIS patchwork, I have, until now, refrained from the first-person singular. If I cannot claim to have been impartial, I have attempted to preserve a third-personal tone. I now propose, as the spymasters used to say, to come into clear. What follows (somewhat edited and occasionally amplified) was first written, in letter form, in the summer of 2014 to my friend, the writer Joseph Epstein of Chicago, with whom I have corresponded for many years.[75]

Dear Joe,

Events in 'the Middle East' have been somewhat loudly ignored in our exchanges, perhaps because there is nothing wise and eloquent or at all new to say about them. You were succinct in your support of Israel and I was/am

---

75 See *Distant Intimacy* (2014) for our correspondence during 2009.

happy to take the same line, that of what football fans call 'a loyal supporter', the kind who, despite any questionable tactics of players and management, continues to yell for our side in good times and in bad, as Babar the elephant puts it. Am I about to play the squeamish part and deplore what Israel has done, is doing and is prepared, it seems, to do again? I *am* squeamish and, no, I am not about to withdraw my support, as if it mattered, except, perhaps, in the great phantom battle that, as usual, attends any evidence that Israel/the Jews (the distinction on which Jacqueline Rose and co. insist serves only to underline the linkage) has/have done anything to defend themselves.

One has only to imagine what the BBC, CNN or Sky News reporter would have said if he or she had been in Hamburg, Berlin, Leipzig or wherever else during the war, when Allied bombers came in and dropped their loads on 'innocent' civilians. Of course, attempts have been made, more or less eloquent, more or less in good faith, to accuse the Allies of being as bad as the Nazis in their 'indiscriminate' bombing; but the ability of the media to play the part of venal Homeric gods, at once in the battle and above it, did not exist until the new technology and the new vocabulary, in which fine feelings of humane meta-Christian sentiments are purveyed by journalists, whose finesse rarely steps outside parameters acceptable to their paymasters.

The British have raised many memorials to their war dead, but were reluctant to do so in the case of Bomber Command; both its higher officers and the crews, of whom about a third, perhaps more, died on their very dangerous missions, were – until very recently – little honoured. What they did seemed callous; the bombs fell alike on the just and the unjust. Few remarked that the Allied raids, justified and effective or not (Albert Speer went against the *bien-pensant* script and confessed that the raids had been greatly disruptive of German production), were *preceded* by quite a long period by the German/Nazi raids on Warsaw, Rotterdam and other targets, which, at the time, were not in 'enemy' territory and were producing nothing to threaten the security of the Reich. However denunciatory, it is noteworthy that none of the revisionists emphasised, or even mentioned, how many *children* died in the Allied raids. Whatever bully-boyishness was implied, the British and the Americans have always been spared the suggestion that they particularly targeted children. It requires no very elaborate analysis of the not-very sub-text to see that the 'blood libel' has been recycled, by nice journalists with humane consciences, to fit today's circumstances.

German indignation at the destruction of Berlin continued into the last days of the war and beyond. As I mention in my autobiography *Going Up*, a clubman friend of mine, who was in Special Forces of some kind, told me in 1981 how:

> Very late in the war, the RAF had bombed two ships, which were at anchor in a Baltic bay. They were, in fact, prison ships with 'displaced persons' on board. After the ships sank, the SS shot any prisoners who managed to swim ashore. Soon afterwards, British commandos captured Schleswig-Holstein; they found dozens of bodies washed up or left on the shore.
>
> The German Field Marshal Milch had surrendered to Tyldesley-Jones (then an acting brigadier) in order to avoid capture by the Russians. Arrogant and bombastic, he insisted that the British and the Germans should have united to destroy the 'Bolshevik savages'.
>
> 'Savages? What about your concentration camps?'
>
> 'For Slavs and such creatures,' Milch said.
>
> 'I want you to come for a walk with me.' The brigadier

led the field marshal to the shore where the bodies had
been heaped by the tide.

'Well?'

'Look closely,' Tyldesley-Jones said. 'Each of these men
was murdered.'

Milch sniffed and bent to inspect the bodies. Each had a
bullet wound in the temple. After he had looked at three or
four, he burst into tears and sat on the wet beach.

This credible (*quia incredibile*) anecdote comes from a man
of no high intelligence, but of a British order of decency and
truthfulness, which may still exist in antique pockets, but has
largely yielded to the fabricators of the shit culture known
as the media. Yes, the Medes did get through, the fanciful
might say, *fra parentesi*, just as Cavafy perceived. The triumph of whatever is said to be 'appropriate', in conduct or
in speech, has led to the meshing of news and comment,
and to the corruption of truth and honesty by columnists
and solemnists, rough and smooth. A recent example, re:
the present hostilities in the Middle East, was sent to me
by an ex-leftist of amiable intentions. A *Guardian* journalist, Jonathan Freedland, claims to be citing an old colleague:
'This conflict is the political equivalent of LSD – distorting

the senses of all those who come into contact with it, and sending them crazy.' He was speaking chiefly of those who debate the issue from afar – the passions that are stirred; the bitterness and loathing that spew forth, especially online, of a kind rarely glimpsed when faraway wars are discussed.

> While an acid trip usually comes in lurid colours, here it induces a tendency to monochrome: one side is pure good, the other pure evil – with not a shade of grey in sight.
>
> But the LSD effect also seems to afflict the participants in the conflict. They too can act crazy, taking steps that harm not only their enemy but themselves. Again and again, their actions are self-defeating.

Good intentions are manifest here, and so is the futility of their expression in falsely analogical terms. LSD is a hallucinatory drug, taken voluntarily, sometimes (so Aldous Huxley claimed) enabling you to see the world in colours more lurid and exhilarating than normal – in Aldous's case, sub-normal – sight can supply. Those who drop acid do occasionally suppose that they can fly, but seldom, if ever, delude themselves into thinking that they are, or possess, rockets with which to destroy their enemies.

The seeming even-handedness of Freedland's anony-
mous source is central to the 'Mercutio complex', a chronic
condition of today's 'median man': the plague he wishes on
both sides makes him the only sane man with his brave head
on the (cushioned) block. It is, generally speaking, more
than his or her life or job is worth to come out clearly with
an *analysis* that goes beyond the enumeration of typical
horrors. Since, as Ed Luttwak has been forthright enough
to say, the Israelis are better trained, have precise targets in
their sights, and – unfair rather – better defences for their
civilian population, it is not surprising that (a) they suffer
fewer casualties and (b) they seem more, yes, callous than
the enemies, whose only ambition is to exterminate them.

Hamas (and its adherents in Europe) would like nothing
better than to do to all Israelis (and all Jews) precisely what
the media like to make out Israel is deliberately doing to
schools, hospitals and that blameless organisation known as
'the UN', whose agencies perpetuate the myth that all that
lies between mankind and happy days is the noxious doctrine of Zionism. The latest student slogan is, in effect, '*Nous
sommes tous des Palestiniens*', translated into whatever the
local language is (I've heard it in Glasgow). The wish to be a
victim doubles with the desire to victimise. As the Cultural

Revolution proved, there is no bully like a young bully with a cause in his sails. Do I go too far? Is it far enough?

Among D. H. Lawrence's least-read books is *Fantasia of the Unconscious.* If the grace of God doesn't hold, or better offers don't come along (oh, that person from Porlock, how we do wonder what keeps him!), I can imagine perpetrating a similar self-certifying number. My reckless book will begin with a recap of Raul Hilberg's callous-seeming study *The Destruction of the European Jews.* It might be foolish enough to make mention of the indifference of the British and the Americans to the actual process of mass murder. How shall we (ah, we!) account for the quantity of their tears and the failure to do anything practical to impede Hitler's crusade? Should we mention how FDR gave the representatives of 'the Jews' just one half an hour of his precious wartime time? Churchill did, at least, and at most, instruct Anthony Eden, his right-hand manikin, to see to it that something was done; but was it? A happy logic, which required all Allied actions to be of military utility, entailed that the gas chambers were no proper target. Yes, yes, old ground.

My fantasia will go on to suggest that the discovery that some Jews had escaped extermination was not the best news that anyone on the victorious side got to hear.

The crudest reaction was that of the new socialist British
Foreign Secretary, handsome Anthony Eden's unhand-
some replacement Ernest Bevin, who – made aware of
the desperate desire of survivors to reach Eretz Israel –
said, 'We're not 'avin' the Jews pushing to the front of the
queue.' The not-all-that-repressed wish was, and is, that
all Jews had disappeared.[76]

The only partially successful Holocaust did, in the
event, have one devastating consequence: Hitler's crusade
against the Jews, whom Martin Luther had marked down
for punitive/exterminatory treatment, was so appalling in
its reluctantly and eventually revealed cruelty that Christianity itself and its God, triune or whatever He/They were
supposed to be, were hauled into question. There was an
attempt to give Christianity some kind of a new look; it
can be seen, for petty instance, in the poster-boy crucifixion painted, in the 1950s, by Graham Sutherland for the
rebuilt Coventry Cathedral, which had been hit by the
ungodly Huns almost certainly because it stood, through

---

76 Fearful of Arab reaction and determined to remain influential in the region, the Attlee
government of 1945 put an embargo on Jewish immigration into Palestine. The British
solution was to send the remnant of Europe's Jews back for distribution among those
who had collaborated in the Holocaust. Neither Britain nor the US allowed more than
a select few Jews to enter their territory. Zionism became the only hope for many survivors. See Jon Kimche, *The Secret Roads* (1955).

no fault of its own, in a heavily industrialised Midland city. Christianity did take a toss in the 1940s. The assumption among post-war planners/hopers of almost all stripes, red or blue or in between, was that religion was not the answer.

Karl Popper's *The Open Society and Its Enemies*, composed during the war, scarcely mentioned religion or God, let alone Allah. It was assumed that civilisation would turn away from the God Whom Mr Eliot did not find strange, and that reason and institutional decency would prevail. History was now bound to be secular. What René Girard says in his *Job* is the same old story about the same old story: the 'scapegoat mechanism' lies (aha!) at the foundation of all societies, civilised or not. The presumption was that the exposure of the arbitrary nature of the 'mechanism' would serve to disempower it.

The singular role of the Jews is, however, so important, so *reliable*, in the language of [western] morals (and of Judaeo-Christianity's parody, Islam) that not even the unabashed, unapologetic militancy of at least some of the Holocaust's survivors (any number of whom were denied access to the US or to the UK) could be allowed for long to render obsolete the role of 'the Jews' in the language of morals and the machinery of Christian self-importance. If

Yeats's centre is to hold, Jews have to be victims: it's in the Book. When they defend themselves, or strike at their enemies, our values are put in question, and Islam's too. Long live the Yellow Star and the 'blood libel' with it. We can then unite in knowing who is to blame. Facts and commentary, history and myth have their double and redoubled helices, twist round each other and provide readings that reinforce and confirm the governing principle.

Cut forward to a slice of contemporary, contemptible life, as conveyed to me by an intellectual/ex-academic close friend. He writes of an often-on-TV personality:

> Talks loudly to be overheard, an utter show-off, with a raucous common laugh that he projects across the room in order to dominate his surroundings. A contemptible swank, as Carthusians and Paulines used to say. He sauntered out of the dining room once or twice, probably to smoke a fag, and glanced sideways with a smirk to judge the effect he made. He was at school with Paul Ettedgui, whom probably you know well from films. Ettedgui and his brother[77] suffered from the last syllable of their sur-

---

77 The brothers' father, Joseph Ettedgui, founded the couture clothing chain Joseph.

name rhyming with their race. Almost every day, Master
X would sidle up behind them and whisper in their ear,
'Gas the lot of them!'

My nutty, meta-Lawrencian book might well be called *In
Earlier Episodes*. It would trace the low dishonesty of the
post-war decades (lowness and dishonesty being by no
means limited to Auden's 1930s) by joining up the dots
re: the fact of and responses to the Holocaust, the creation
of the European Union and the 'crusader' state of Israel.
It will not be a work of history but a psychic profile of
what has not been said about the underlying, especially
European, subconscious and the return of the repressed
and/or the end of remission.

The Franco-German rapprochement, represented not
long ago by François Hollande holding hands with the
gentlemanly German President, presumably because *la*
Merkel was too busy, is a vestige of the whole, honourable,
businesslike attempt, inaugurated by the unimpeachable,
impeccable Robert Schuman and Jean Monnet, to ensure
that the Great War III would never take place between
European powers. Amalgamation was a small price to pay
and might yield big dividends, including the obliteration

of antique antagonisms. Post-1945 Europeans planned, consciously, to get rich, after which all other things, moral lustre included, would be added unto them.

At the same time, but never admittedly, guilt re: the Holocaust had to be found a place under the heavy, tightly woven carpet that became the European Union. Nothing wrong with this noble endeavour, except that it insisted that the lion was not only going to lie down with the lamb, or the sheep, but also that there were no lions and no sheep, but some new animal altogether – the European goodybeest. Henceforth, there would be neither north nor south; neither east nor west (and we will never again mention Aryans). The Treaty of Rome created a secular pseudo-Catholicism, in which we would not talk bawdy, as Robert Walpole recommended, so that all might join in, but rather make money, which doesn't smell, though a lotta humans seem to have a nose for it. Economics would create the homogenised, pacific European creed, which neither nationality nor religion had ever generated. Even the 1968 students bought into altogether boyishness by shouting: '*Nous sommes tous des Juifs allemands.*' Meaning, no, they weren't, but they'd like victim status and the attendant perks.

The replacement of 'race' by allegiance to an ideal of unity had a certain precedent in the US. Whether or not Lincoln's war was legally justified or on the side of progress, it tore the US in half and then put it together, with rough stitches, in a way that, whatever the scars and occasional rips, seemed to hold. Why spoil the party by remarking that, under the star-spangled banner, all deep divisions remained? The long humiliation of black Americans being beyond dispute; it is ignoble to argue about who had the worse deal, historically – Jews or blacks. It is of the nature of such matters that, in the US, the two pariah groups should, at first, make some kind of common cause. In the 1930s, at least, Jews supplied the cutting edginess – Dorothy Parker's, for instance, in those happy old days – and the legal savvy. This is not to say that there were no clever or fine black voices – Paul Robeson's, not least – but Yankee Jews were able to claim, with justice, to be speaking for a principle, not for themselves, which was convenient as well as true.

What happened later – cue the glorious '60s! – was that black emancipation declared itself, first by denouncing the most accessible, least dangerous of its enemies, i.e. its allies, the Jews. Blacks would not be mature, free-standing men until they dared to turn and rend their false 'fathers'. Poor rich Lenny Bernstein famously attempted to keep the alliance going by paying 'reparations', but some blacks at least were not about to relinquish their new licence to enjoy the fresh airing of an age-old prejudice.

Anti-Israelism became kosher after the 1967 war, when de Gaulle said of the Jews (not the Israelis) that they were *'un peuple d'élite, sûr de lui-même et dominateur'* (an elite people, sure of itself and dominating). The new anti-Semitism sprang, as anti-Israelism, from the horse's nose. Comedy and tragedy go *bras-dessus, bras-dessous* in this utterance. With regard to the last two 'accusations', that Jews were 'sure of themselves and dominating', de Gaulle might as well have been speaking of himself (how he wished that all three allegations were still true of France!). Indeed, *le grand* Charles affected surprise when Raymond Aron, who had rallied to de Gaulle in London in 1940, broke with him on account of what he claimed had been a 'compliment'. He told the truth, he lied; de Gaulle was, in fact, outraged that the Israelis had made a pre-emptive attack on, in particular, Egyptian airfields against his specific injunction. The Israelis' main weapon of attack during those decisive raids was the French Mirage fighter, which de Gaulle then ceased, officially at least, to export to them. De Gaulle had an atavistic 'fear' of *les Juifs*, which went back, on narrow-gauge twin tracks, to St Louis's Catholicism and Charles Maurras's *Action française*. The comedy was that de Gaulle had complained, back in 1941, that 'more Jews than Frenchmen' rallied to his call from London.

Between 1948 (when the Arabs failed, despite British encouragement, to strangle the little circumcised Heracles in its tight cradle) and 1967, Israel had been almost every European's gallant little power, surrounded by enemies who outnumbered and threatened at any moment to engulf it. The French and British, splendidly and ingloriously in character, saw nothing wrong in making use of Israel in 1956 in order to fabricate a righteous excuse for invading Egypt. That embarrassing (because futile) episode confirmed Israelis in the traditional Jewboyish role of underlings who could sometimes be let usefully out of their box, as long as they could then be folded back into it again (sidebar: the slaves who died at the Battle of Marathon were buried in a separate heap from true-born Athenians, but thanks all the same).

Post the 1967 victory, Israel failed, as moralists hasten to say, to return the 'occupied territories' to their proper owners. The boundaries had, in truth, been set quite recently, and arbitrarily, by the French and the British after the so-called Arab uprising of 1915, its spontaneity primed with much British gold. After their failure to withdraw, the new unapologetic Jews became pariahs of a slightly different stripe; but it was a left-wing comfort to be able to say that they *hadn't changed.* The difficulty and the difference was that sufferance was not at all the Israelis' style of badge. Having no sense of shame, they did not yield the pavement, as Freud's father did, to the out-of-my-way Gentile.

The *New York Review of Books*, and its cousin the *London Review of Books*, evolved a meta-version of the schism that divided US Jews and blacks. To prove how emancipated, outspoken and unintimidated by dated loyalties they were, the editors and attendant in-group, *quelques Juifs compris*, demonstrated their fearlessness by becoming de facto anti-Semites. You can't get more emancipated, Jewwise, than that. In this way, the in-crowd could be brave and not risk the slightest bloody nose, although mutually scratched backs were not uncommon. Flashback and you'll find that there were Jews for Adolf, early on; and now there were New Yorkers for Edward Said, and, yes, sir, Arafat.

First Zionism and then Israel had had certain useful-
ness for the European powers until 1967. In line with the
classic recipe during and after the Great War, the British
divided the Middle East – it was closer to Whitehall in
those days and was known as 'the Near East' – into fac
titious 'countries', whose instability would make them
easier to supervise. The victorious Europeans also broke
up the Ottoman Empire – with spiteful officiousness,
according to Elie Kedourie – and turned most of the Fertile
Crescent (London and Paris called it, quietly, 'the loot')
into 'occupied territories' on a very big scale. Swathes
of land were then divided by dotted lines and allotted to
handsome fellows with big teeth and robed pedigrees who
were posted as kings in more-or-less ungovernable territories with incompatible inhabitants. Hence the need for
a managerial British 'mandate' for Palestine.

The notion of a 'national home' for the Jews had been
mooted, in 1917, by the first-class-minded A. J. Balfour, less
out of Christian concern for persecuted Jews than for fear
that 'Jewish finance' – the usual, overrated, many-armed,
Argus-eyed bogeyman of anti-Semitic fancy – would short
the Allies and put its *gelt* on Germany. Once the central
powers were disempowered, Balfour's promise had to be

kept, unfortunately; the British were still that honourable, if they really had to be. Some new Jews were admitted
to Palestine. Fortunately, not all that many wanted to go.
Thus, the Arabs were rewarded, big time, and menaced very
gently, in order to keep them glad to have the British there
to blow officious whistles and pump oil at discount rates.

In one of your letters, you coined a great phrase: 'The
Good Intentions Paving Company'. President Woodrow
Wilson is surely its founding father and the greatest political
quack of almost our time. Nothing was better intended or, in
the event, more poisonous than his recipe for European pac-
ification, self-determination. What snake did he get that oil
from? Its salesman assumed that the world was composed
of 'peoples' who had been cruelly divided, by imperial con-
glomerates (the Austro-Hungarians in particular), and thus
denied their natural right to self-expressive self-government.
W. Wilson's good intentions issued licences to huff-and-
puffers, greatish or petty, to lay claim to the 'leadership' of
'nations' that had previously, more-or-less sulkily, sometimes happily, co-existed. The Europe of racist ranters and
raving revanchists was not far to seek. The only people who
were not allowed to be 'self-determining' were the Jews.
No one had liked them before, but now they were included

out for economic, political, as well as the ongoing religious reasons; fuck me twice over time. Plus they were Bolsheviks; make that three times for luck.

It is, of course, extra-curricular to blame anyone but the Germans for the Holocaust, and somewhat bad history, in terms of practical, murderous enterprise. All the bloody same, quite a number of willingly ancillary folk, Ukrainians not least, were implicated, even if they now want out of the index. Today's Ukraine, scanned as psycho-history, again illustrates the principle that the first enemy should be the weakest enemy. In the 1930s, the Ukrainians were starved in large numbers by Stalin and that nice Mr Khrushchev (who put Uncle Joe in the dock as soon as the latter was dead), which gave them occasion, under the Nazi aegis, to recover their manliness by massacring unarmed Jews. Now, the meta-Wilsonian 'self-determination' number allows Russian-speakers to claim a right to, yes, dependent independence: they clamour for V. Putin esquire kindly to put his arm through theirs and his foot on their fellow citizens' necks. The old schizo-number runs again: Ukrainians prove how Russian they are by a willingness to shoot other Ukrainians.

A British general (name can be checked somewhere)

told Golda Meir, in post-war Jerusalem, that 'the Jews' must have done *something* to deserve (key word) the fate they suffered in the war. She turned quite nasty, sources tell us, at the 'innocent' suggestion that, as very usual, the Jews, deep down, surely had only themselves to blame. Refusal to accept responsibility, whether for Jesus's death or the Black Death or whatever else you have on the charge sheet, is part of what makes the Israelis so embarrassing, not least to civilised, out-of-range Jews, who, in the standard figure, prefer co-religionists who do not make waves.

The present condition of Europe is, in my never-to-be-published view, the consequence of post-1945 decades of false-consciousness, in which illusions of common culture, common purposes, common values, even, have been fostered in a grandiose attempt to make European history begin again *after* the *Shoah*. Statisticians and economists, our new masters of the world's game and gamble, are expert at deciding at which point the new analysis will begin, and the figures are made to conform to some preconceived scheme. The whitening of the European sepulchre (an intelligent revision of René Girard's 'scapegoat mechanism') need not have been a conscious consideration *chez* Monnet and Schuman; but would the attempt at para-national amalgamation ever have even somewhat succeeded if it had not supplied a great mantle of forgetfulness and self-forgiving?

The only trouble, some might say, is that an inconvenient number of Jews survived what 'we' arranged in order to consign the bad old Europe to the oubliette. Here's the scarcely buried sub-text: whatever may be said about the folly or otherwise of her policies, Israel now stands as an irritant, an unapologetic assertion that the Jews will not do what's best for them and, oh, 'us', and ... go quietly. The European need is for the myth to be redeemed: let them – the Jews – do something *typically* unforgivable, especially kill children, and we will then be let off history's hook because the Holocaust will become retrospectively justified and, of course, the fault of 'the Jews'.

Frederic Raphael